The Surrender and the Singing

The Surrender and the Singing

Happiness Through Letting Go

Ray Ashford

WINSTON PRESS

Cover design: Terry Dugan

Library of Congress Catalog Card Number: 84-52501

ISBN: 0-86683-964-X

Printed in the United States of America

5 4 3 2 1

Winston Press, Inc.
430 Oak Grove
Minneapolis, Minnesota 55403

ACKNOWLEDGMENTS

Grateful acknowledgment is made to the following publishers for permission to reprint copyrighted material:

Excerpt from *The Broken Heart*, by James J. Lynch. Copyright © 1977 and reprinted by permission of Basic Books, Inc.

Excerpts from *Turning*, by Emilie Griffin. Copyright © 1980 by Emilie Griffin. Reprinted by permission of Doubleday and Company, Inc.

Excerpt from *A Spiritual Autobiography*, by William Barclay. Copyright © 1977 and reprinted by permission of William B. Eerdmans Publishing Co.

Excerpt from "One Blinding Moment," by Elizabeth Byrd. Reprinted by permission of Guideposts Magazine. Copyright © 1967 by Guideposts Associates, Inc., Carmel, New York 10512.

Excerpts from *The Four Loves*, by C. S. Lewis. Copyright © 1960 by Helen Joy Lewis. Reprinted by permission of Harcourt Brace Jovanovich, Inc.

Excerpt from *The Prophet*, by Kahlil Gibran. Copyright © 1955 and reprinted by permission of Alfred A. Knopf, Inc.

Excerpts from *Hearts That We Broke Long Ago*, by Merle Shain. Copyright © 1983 and reprinted by permission of the Canadian publisher, McClelland and Stewart Limited.

Excerpts from *The Courage to Create*, by Rollo May. Copyright © 1975. Also excerpts from *The Mind Alive*, by Harry and Bonaro Overstreet. Copyright © 1954. Reprinted by permission of W. W. Norton, Inc.

Excerpts from *Gift from the Sea*, by Anne Morrow Lindbergh. Copyright © 1955 and reprinted by permission of Pantheon Books and Chatto & Windus.

"Even—" from *The Unicorn and Other Poems*, by Anne Morrow Lindbergh. Copyright © 1956 and reprinted by permission of Random, Knopf, Pantheon, Inc.

English translation of "Early Breakfast" by Jacques Prévert, as found in *Jacques Prévert*, by William E. Baker. Copyright © 1967 and reprinted by permission of Twayne Publishers, a division of G. K. Hall & Co., Boston.

Excerpt from *After the Fall*, by Arthur Miller. Copyright © 1964 and reprinted by permission of Viking Penguin Inc.

Excerpt from *For God's Sake, Be Human*, by John Killinger. Copyright © 1970 and reprinted by permission of Word Books, Publishers, Waco, Texas 76796.

Scripture quotations in this publication are from the *Revised Standard Version Common Bible*, copyright © 1973 by the Division of Christian Education of the National Council of the Churches of Christ in the U.S.A. Used by permission.

CONTENTS

PREFACE

Inching along in a queue on a raw March morning, I couldn't help but overhear a conversation between two men standing behind me. "I figure," said one, "if I had another fifty bucks a week, I'd have it made; I'd be on Easy Street."

It is a common assumption: If only we had a little *More* (of whatever it is we seek), life would be clear sailing under cloudless skies.

For centuries, though, the sages and saints have insisted that the way to be rich is to be poor. However unlikely it seems, they say, happiness lies not in addition but in subtraction; happiness lies in relinquishment, in giving up, in letting go; happiness lies in the Less, which through some mysterious alchemy is converted into More.

What follows is reflections, grouped in chapters and interpolated with words of wit and wisdom from a hundred sources, on some of those aspects of life we tend to clutch too tightly and carry too far: roles, stances, and attitudes we need to relinquish before we, and others as well, can be the persons that Love intends.

I leave it to you, my reader, to fill in the gaps in the text with your own observations and so advance the dialogue on which our humanity depends.

1

"I LIKE MY WRINKLES"

I remember three events, all tinged with trauma, that occurred within weeks of each other.

First, I turned fifty. Turning thirty had been easy. Nothing to it. Forty, similarly, had been no problem. But fifty? No. Fifty was different, much different. Fifty seemed over the hill. Fifty, however you sliced it, was *old*.

Compounding my distress, I became a grandfather for the first time. I had been a father for close to thirty years—I was used to that. But a grandfather? I could scarcely believe it. All of a sudden, it seemed, I had moved into the ranks of the patriarchs.

Next I went into a large department store to buy myself a shirt. Uncertain of the size of the one I wanted, I asked the saleswoman for permission to try it on. "Sure," she said, "the changing rooms are right over there." I went into one of the little cubicles, stripped myself to the waist, and was appalled by what I saw. Perhaps it was the three-way mirror, perhaps the harsh lighting coming down from straight overhead. But whatever the case, I looked downright aged. All that crepey skin, all those wrinkles and flab! I was no longer young. The evidence was irrefutable.

I suspect it is true of us all: Our awareness of aging is not so much a gentle, day-by-day feeling of gradual decline as it is a succession of random, jolting realizations of diminished powers.

A heart attack perhaps, a first-time-ever experience of impotence, a rejection in favor of some younger person—aren't these the moments that say to us, brutally sometimes, "You are no longer young"?

> Age takes hold of us by surprise.[1]
>
> —Johann Wolfgang von Goethe

I see young people laughing, reckless, exuberant, and there sweeps over me a wave of the most poignant nostalgia, triggered, I suspect, by a host of memories deeply stored, memories of abilities and moments once enjoyed: memories of the parties and dances, each glowing with a special excitement and promise; memories of the team sports and all the impromptu fun, the sandlot ball games and the touch football in the park; memories of the summer evenings with the sound of the orchestra drifting across the lake; memories of the cross-country skiing, myself bare to the waist, under the warm springtime sun; memories of the power and speed, the springiness and elasticity, the stamina and drive—yes, and memories of being noticed by the girls, the lissome, beautiful girls for whom I am now just another grey anonymous face in the crowd.

> We watch the shifting planes of our face—what was once taut sags, and what was once full becomes taut—the coarsening of the skin and the change in its colouring—the droop of muscles which tiredness and tension inflict upon us. It is interesting, but bewildering, too, because it changes one's external identity. One is no longer the girl that boys whistled at in the street. Prettiness is no more than a ghost, the ghost of a taste (now no more than a ghost) that is left behind when a fine wine has been left too long in the bottle. One will never be noticeable any more.[2]
>
> —Monica Furlong

I miss the advantages of youth, yes, but at the same time I find that middle age has some soaring compensations.

Specifically, I am more confident now, more at ease with people, and certainly more contented. Gone are the furious passions and oppressive ambitions of earlier days. Goals now are more modest, more realistic; and perhaps because of that, life is more calm and serene. More mellow.

I find, too, that I am more independent than I used to be, less victimized by all the social pressures to which a younger humanity is subject. I had a colleague who used to refer to his tranquilizers as his DGD pills. DGD, I learned, stands for Don't-Give-a-Damn. Well, even without the pills, I care much less now about what people think. I am more my own person.

Another blessed advantage of middle age, for some of us at least, is a certain financial freedom. Back when our children were young, Phyl and I, like so many parents of small children, were largely housebound. Our budget provided for some babysitting and a little travel, but not much. Most evenings, weekends, and vacations were spent at home. But today? A different story. We are far more mobile, more free.

I am sure, though, that the greatest changes have been not in outward circumstances but in the interior life, including my capacity for feeling. Once, years ago, I was a little (or more than a little) cool and remote, someone who dealt with life—and with people—in a much too intellectual, impersonal way. But that has changed. Love is now far more freely expressed, as is laughter. Poetry speaks as it never did before, and tears are far closer to the surface, triggered by everything from a farewell party to a Bach fugue.

John Hall Wheelock, the poet, said on his ninetieth birthday, "I've always wanted to live long. I had a lot of work I wanted to do. In old age, things become more intense rather than less so. Things get more poignant—so many associations—everything reverberating with everything else. You don't feel you are any older, but suddenly you realize you are. But instead of life getting dimmer and duller, it gets so poignant it's unbearable. Like looking at the sun, you can't stand it because it's unbearable."[3]

I have a long way to go before I reach ninety, if indeed I ever do. But perhaps because time is so relentlessly running out, I, too, am finding life more brilliant and intense, more poignant and sweet. Or, more accurately, bittersweet. For beyond these beautiful September years, I realize, there are October, November, December; there are the mists, the fading, the sleep. Yet beyond all that again, I believe, there is January; there is some transcendent beginning.

I like my wrinkles.[4]

—Audrey Hepburn

But because January is questionable, while summer or fall, as the case may be, is a distressing reality, some of us do all we can to anchor ourselves in the middle years of our lives. We buy lotions, skin creams, wrinkle removers. We see to it that our slang is current, our wardrobes trendy. We arrange for face-lifts and tummy tucks, hair transplants and dye jobs. We spend hours under the sunlamp or in the sauna, going from there into diet and exercise programs that border on sheer masochism.

Our heroics are understandable and, to some extent, applaudable. After all, aging should be resisted—up to a point. But when that point is passed, the results are, as Marya Mannes put it, "in woman, obscene; in man—pathetic."

Mae West. Aged eighty plus. But grotesquely powdered and painted, still an ash blonde, still bedecked in the black, maraboa-trimmed robe and still parading a crude, vestigial sexuality. A sad sight.

(Sainte-Beuve: "There are people whose watch stops at a certain hour and who remain permanently at that age."[5])

I think also of a man I knew, a frail old gentleman who back in World War I had served in one of the more glamorous branches of the armed forces. It was the high point of his life. Nothing later had even come close. A conversation with him could begin on any of a thousand topics, but always, always it came back to those splendid, triumphant days when he had done battle with the grey-helmeted Hun.

Again it was a case of arrested development and again immensely sad—sad because to live in the past is to commit the serious error of denying the fundamental reality of the present and rejecting life as it is, the only life we have, in favor of some pathetic illusion.

> I don't hold with them [face-lifts]. I'm told by people who've had it done that you always feel like you have a mask on. Women who keep after their faces until they look like saucers automatically lose their character. Anything permanent tends to disappear under the façade.
>
> When you reach an age where you have wrinkles, let your character take over. That's what you have got that is solid.[6]
>
> —Anita Loos

Cornaro, the sixteenth-century Venetian nobleman, wrote in his mid-eighties, "I think my present age, although it is very advanced, the pleasantest and the finest of my life. I would not exchange my age and my life for the most flourishing youthfulness."[7]

Justice Oliver Wendell Holmes, I am told, said at the age of ninety, "This is a great age, the best time of my life. I would advise you all to hurry up and get here as soon as you possibly can."

Justice Felix Frankfurter cabled Thornton Wilder on the occasion of Wilder's sixtieth birthday: DEAR THORNTON WELCOME TO THE GREAT DECADES. FELIX.[8]

I see them among my friends and acquaintances, people who are reveling in "the great decades." I see Mary and Anna, Flo and Irene. I see Charlie and Clair and Vic—all of them people for whom old age is prime time, the best time of their lives.

I have asked them, "Do you ever think you'd like to be young again?"

Their unanimity is amazing: "No. I like where I am. In fact, I've never enjoyed life more."

She was blind, diabetic, and, with one leg amputated at the hip, confined to a wheelchair for the last fifteen years of her life. She spent those years raising thousands upon thousands of dollars for charitable causes. She did it by selling stockings, magazines, Christmas cards—whatever she could arrange to sell by phone.

She never traded upon her handicaps. Most of her customers, in fact, didn't know she was blind. What they did recognize, though, was the voice—warm, gentle, beautiful—and behind it a rare spirit. Here, they sensed, was someone for whom profits were only incidental, someone who never failed to inquire into their lives, their dreams, their needs, someone who genuinely cared and whose every call gladdened their hearts.

She died at the age of seventy-two, and her death, like her life, was a triumph. A downtown church, seating close to 1,000, was filled to capacity with people who remembered her as one of the finest human beings they had ever known.

Apropos are the words of Nietzsche: "He who has a *why* to live can bear with almost any *how*."[9]

Happiness, it seems, is largely dependent on having a goal, a purpose, a cause. People, including the elderly, who have a good reason for living, people who are blessed with some governing purpose, preferably unselfish, are also blessed with meaning and satisfaction.

I see it in the lives of seniors I know; I see them investing their lives in a wide assortment of worthwhile enterprises and in the process having, literally, the time of their lives.

I call on a ninety-five-year-old woman who keeps house for her working daughter. She, the mother, greets me at the door. "Come in, come in! I've just finished scrubbing the kitchen floor. We'll have a cup of tea." Scrubbing the floor! At age ninety-five? "Yes, it keeps me young."

I think she would agree: What really keeps her young is being useful, busy, needed.

I visit a hospital for the chronically ill. I hear a man singing, beautifully. A high sweet tenor that floats down the hall. "Who's that?" I ask one of the nurses. "Oh, that's an elderly man who comes in every Wednesday afternoon and sings for the patients, all their favorite songs. They love it." I don't meet the singer but I am sure that he, too, is a happy man. He has a purpose, a cause.

Hokusai, the great Japanese artist, wrote, "From the age of six I had a mania for drawing the form of things. By the time I was fifty I had published an infinity of designs; but all I produced before the age of seventy is not worth taking into account. At seventy-three I learned a little about the real structure of nature, animals, plants, trees, birds, fishes, and insects. In consequence, when I am eighty I shall penetrate the mystery of things; at one hundred I shall certainly have reached a marvelous stage; and when I am one hundred and ten, everything I do, be it a dot or a line, will be alive. I beg those who live as long as I to see if I do not keep my word."[10]

I am convinced that people like Hokusai, people possessed by some towering purpose, tend to live a long time and, more important, to *live* as long as they live.

> There is only one solution if old age is not to be an absurd parody of our former life, and that is to go on pursuing ends that give our existence a meaning—devotion to individuals, to groups or causes, social, political, intellectual, or creative work.[11]
>
> —Simone de Beauvoir

Cervantes, who had been a professional soldier, was almost sixty when he began *Don Quixote*, acclaimed by many as the greatest novel of all time. Cervantes completed the work at sixty-eight.

Thomas Hardy's greatest period was his last, and his finest poetry was written between the ages of seventy-five and eighty-five.

At eighty-one Goethe finished *Faust*, and at eighty-two Churchill completed *A History of the English-Speaking Peoples*.

Verdi capped his career at eighty with *Falstaff*, his most adventurous opera, and was still composing at eighty-five.

Ralph Vaughan Williams also did some superb work in the eighth and ninth decades of his life.

Andres Segovia was performing in his eighties before sellout audiences all over the world.

Arthur Rubinstein gave one of his greatest recitals in Carnegie Hall at the age of eighty-nine, and Arturo Toscanini continued to conduct with great authority until close to his death at the age of ninety.

Corot was about eighty when he painted his most accomplished pictures, Franz Hals eighty-five when he reached his pinnacle. Giovanni Bellini was acknowledged at eighty-six to be the finest painter in Venice.

At eighty-eight, Michelangelo drew the architectural plans for the Church of Santa Maria degli Angeli. Monet, Renoir, Cézanne, Matisse, Picasso, Cassatt, Braque, Rouault, John, Benton, Pissarro, Gainsborough, O'Keeffe, and Chagall were others who painted superbly at an advanced age.

Grandma Moses began painting at seventy-two and was still going strong at 100.

Galileo did his most important work in his seventies. Edison remained active and productive until eighty-three. Pavlov continued the research begun in his youth until he was in his early eighties, adding to it all the time.

Alfred North Whitehead's four major works were produced in the twenty years that followed his enforced retirement, at age sixty-five, from the English academic scene.

Marshal Tito, in his mid-eighties, was a powerful head of state, and George Meany, also in his eighties, dominated the AFL-CIO with its fourteen million members. At eighty-eight,

Konrad Adenauer served as chancellor of West Germany, and at ninety-one, Eamon de Valera was president of Ireland.

At eighty-five, Coco Chanel headed her own fashion design firm. At eighty-nine, Mary Baker Eddy was directing the Christian Science Church.

Albert Schweitzer headed a hospital in Africa at the age of eighty-nine. John XXIII, that most influential of pontiffs, was seventy-eight when he began his papacy. Clara Barton, founder of the Red Cross, was ninety and still working fourteen hours a day. "While the strength is given me," she said, "I have no right to lay it down."

> If many older adults fretted less about the unavailable years and analysed the amount of relaxed time available to them, they would be astonished at the treasure which the years of later and late adulthood have delivered to them. Hundreds of creative ideas of every kind grow in the soil of relaxed time and the relaxed contemplative mind.[12]
>
> —John A. B. MacLeish

I had always admired A. J. Casson's paintings but never met him until quite recently, when I heard him speak. In his mid-eighties, white haired and slight, he captivated us by his essential goodness. Not surprisingly, I suppose, I found the artist much like his art, clean and quiet and warm. Beautiful.

"I can't understand," he said, and in all sincerity, "why people pay such large sums for my paintings. I sometimes question their judgment.

"But at the same time," he added, half smiling, "I can't help but be grateful."

He went on to enumerate some of his reasons for gratitude: He had his wife, his health, and a host of rich memories; he could still drive his car and still "paint a pretty good picture." He was of all men the most blessed.

As I listened to him, it occurred to me that the distinction between doing and being is often artificial, for in many instances the two go hand in hand: The celebrity, honored for his achievements, is also a superb human *be*ing.

It struck me, too, as it has before, that right here is one of the greatest services the elderly can render: They can exemplify the human ideal. By the very quality of their lives they can point us to the stars.

I visited an elderly friend. "I feel so useless," she lamented. "I'm not doing anything, not accomplishing anything. I'm just limping along from day to day." I reminded her that she has dozens of friends who cherish her, people like myself who glow in her warmth, her wit, her joy. I pointed out to her—truly—that what she does for us is incalculable and that she does it by what she is, a benediction and a delight.

> As for old age, embrace and love it. It abounds with pleasure if you know how to use it. The gradually declining years are among the sweetest in a man's life; and I maintain that even when they have reached the extreme limit, they have their pleasure still.[13]
>
> —Seneca

2

NONPOSSESSIVE PARENTS

He had a dreadful childhood. His grandmother was insane. His father committed suicide. His mother, a coarse and promiscuous woman, despised her son and ended up, in a towering rage, pitching him down the stairs and out of the house.

He never forgave her. In fact, he never went near her again. He was Schopenhauer, the philosopher.

Item: On July 5, 1980, the *Ottawa Journal* ran a front-page headline: PARENTS DON'T WANT DAUGHTER BACK. Three hours of pleading with the parents of a west end teenager, the *Journal* reported, yielded nothing but the firm statement, "She's 16 and on her own." Suzanne had not been in trouble with the police. She was a good student. She was described as a nice, level-headed girl by everyone who knew her. But she was an adult according to law, her parents said, a free agent. They had kicked her out because they'd planned on only one child; Suzanne was a second child, unwanted from the start. They had done their duty as parents, and now it was time for her to make her own way in the world. Suzanne's father and mother are both top-level civil servants. They live in a fashionable Ottawa suburb, and between them they earn about $135,000 a year.

Item: When Sally was 13, her mother, a family therapist, remarried. Before long Sally felt like an unwanted boarder in the house in an Ontario town where her mother lived with her new husband, a high school principal. She ran away. Her mother didn't bother to inform the police that she was missing. Sure now of her mother's rejection, Sally fled to another Ontario town where her father and his new wife ran a small business. Her father made her welcome in a halfhearted way, but her stepmother was afraid she would wreck their marriage. Since then, Sally's life has been a succession of foster homes, group homes and street life. Sometimes on her birthday or on Mother's Day she calls her mom and asks to come home. Last year, on Sally's 16th birthday, her mother consented to a visit. Sally slept in the living room because the bedrooms in the house belonged to her two toddler stepsisters. She noticed that the family photos in the house didn't include her. Sally's mother tells her she can come home to live "when you get your act together." Sally, lonely and embittered, has a recurrent fantasy: to walk in on one of her mother's family therapy sessions.

Item: In May 1981, Brian, 16, had a row with his parents. They kicked him out of their home in Etobicoke, Ontario. Two weeks later, Brian, contrite and repentant, returned home. A note was posted on the door: "We've moved to Alberta. Have a good life."[1]

—Loral Dean

On the one hand: parents who can scarcely wait to be rid of their children, even to the extent of throwing them right out of the house.

On the other: parents who find it extremely difficult to let go of their offspring. Clutching, overprotective parents . . .

"Forget it, Jennifer. Nice party or not, I don't want you out after dark."

"No, Joel, summer camp is out of the question. Maybe when you're a little older."

"Skis for Christmas? No way. I'm afraid you'd break your neck."

"No, Danny, we've discussed it, your father and I, and we see no point in sending you off to university a thousand miles away when there's a perfectly good one right here at home."

It is understandable: We are twenty to forty years older than our offspring, we have seen far more of the world, including the hurts it can inflict, and we don't want to see them go out and get hurt.

I notice, though, that often we fail to recognize that our children are no longer children.

A distinguished middle-aged educator observes wryly, "Here I am, crowding fifty, but to my mother I'm still a child. Every time I'm with her it's the same old refrain. 'Eat a good breakfast, David.' 'Dress warmly.' 'Get to bed in good time.' Just as if I were nine!"

He muses, "Do parents ever stop being parents? Do they ever relinquish responsibility for their children, ever free them to either sink or swim?"

In some instances, let's face it, it is simple selfishness that gets in the way of our letting go.

We dread old age, some of us. Its potential for loneliness, poverty, and decrepitude can cloud our whole horizon.

"But," we remind ourselves (at a deep level), "there's insurance against all that. I have the children."

We don't, of course, say baldly, "I want you to stay home and look after me." But we do get the message across in other ways.

We drop hints: "I hear Bessie Smith's daughter and son-in-law have taken her into their home. Isn't that nice! So much better than Sunset Villa!"

We bribe our offspring. One couple I know did it by building "the kids" a house next door.

We feign illness and in the process say implicitly, "It's your duty to take good care of me."

Many are the ways in which we point out to our children that they are their parents' keepers.

True, we no longer have custom on our side, as our forebears did back in the days when children were expected to stay home and run the family farm, carry on the family business, or take over the old family home, with its three floors and eleven rooms, and set the old folks up in comfortable quarters on the main floor. Society now expects its young people to strike out on their own. But even so, there are parents who defy the trend by seeing to it that their offspring never leave the nest.

I think of people I know. Parents who in denying their children freedom are also denying them challenge, growth, fulfillment, joy. Parents who are stunting and impairing their children's lives.

She was middle-aged and unmarried, her face drawn with tension. Her days were spent in an office, her evenings and weekends at home taking care of an ailing elderly mother. "I'm an only child," she explained. "If I don't take care of her. . . ."

Earlier she had said, "I don't know why I'm here," but bit by bit the picture emerged. From time to time she had come close to leaving home and making a life of her own, but always there was something that prevented her departure. Her mother was laid low by back problems. Or was having heart trouble. Or was in depression.

At first there were only hints of the anger she felt, and with every hint there was an apology: "I must admit, there are times when I get a little irritated with my mother. I wish she weren't quite so demanding. But that isn't right, I know. I should be more sympathetic."

We talked several times, and the more we talked, the more her anger surfaced.

Finally there was an explosion. "I hate her! She's a mean, selfish old bitch. I have no home of my own, no husband, no kids, and it's all because of her! I hate her, I hate her! What am I going to do?" She sobbed uncontrollably.

> In the town where I was born lived a woman and her daughter, who walked in their sleep. One night, while silence enfolded the world, the woman and her daughter, walking, yet asleep, met in the mist-veiled garden. And the mother spoke and she said: "At last, at last, my enemy! You by whom my youth was destroyed—who have built up your life upon the ruins of mine! Would I could kill you!" And the daughter spoke, and she said: "O hateful woman, selfish and old! Who stands between my freer self and me! Who would have my life an echo of your own faded life! Would you were dead!" At the moment a cock crew, and both women awoke. The mother said gently, "Is that you, darling?" And the daughter answered gently, "Yes, dear!"[2]
>
> —Kahlil Gibran

Winnifred Bryce, a longtime family friend, once said something my parents were fond of quoting, perhaps because it was so completely in accord with their own convictions. "Parents," said Winnifred, "should exercise a little judicious neglect."

Like Winnifred, my mother and father were devout believers in hands-off parenting, with the result that, along with my brothers, I was given an extraordinary amount of freedom.

I could roam all over the city and countryside, could go out camping in the mountains, could, as a teenager, be away from home for days or even weeks at a stretch.

I could hop freights, climb dizzy heights, ride motorcycles, set out swimming solo across long stretches of open water. I could be—and was—brought home bloody and concussed, bones broken and faculties impaired. But almost never did I hear the usual admonitions and prohibitions: Easy! Be careful! Watch out! Don't—you'll hurt yourself!

People may have concluded that my parents didn't care. Not so. They did care. Immensely. But they never confused caring with overprotectiveness.

> Like Harry Truman, Franklin Roosevelt had, in the words of a recent biographer, Joseph Alsop, "an immensely happy childhood." He genuinely adored his mother, then and ever after, and her doting did not exclude a degree of freedom and adventure for, as she put it, her "instinctively good little boy." Once, when he was 5, he became uncharacteristically gloomy; nothing seemed to please him. So after consulting his father, she told Franklin that he could do whatever he wished for an entire day. He did, returning dirty and exhausted. She never asked where he had been or what he'd done.[3]
>
> —David McCullough

"I'm in a power struggle with my child," she said. "I'm not giving an inch."

I know her son. I know something of his frustration and hostility. "I wish," he seethes, "my mother would get off my back!" He wants—and deserves—to spread his wings and fly.

I felt like saying to her, "Look, if you don't ease up a little, if you don't relinquish some of your authority, you're going to have a real problem on your hands. You may even lose him entirely."

Love is not grasping, possessive, demanding. On the contrary, love relinquishes, releases; love lets go.

Love does not, of course, reject. It does not evict or dislodge, does not drive out and away. Nor does it desert and abandon.

Love's timing is right. Love neither lets go too soon nor hangs on too long. Love walks the middle, balanced way between two kinds of selfishness: the selfishness that says, "I won't let you go," and the equal selfishness that says, "Out! I can't be bothered with you."

I know ambitious people who applied great pressure to their children and thereby made life downright miserable for all concerned. (In some instances the pressure was counterproductive; sons and daughters failed, and children and parents alike considered themselves disgraced.)

On the other hand, I know people who waived their parental hopes and did so with amazing equanimity.

Jason, my friend, came out of a humble background and went on to become a distinguished scientist, a man whose work now takes him all over the world. Like all parents, Jason has dreams for his children. He wants them to be highly educated, accomplished, successful. But, much to his credit, he sits lightly on those expectations.

Jason's son Brian was a good student, but in high school, unfortunately, he soured on education. "I just can't hack it," he said. "Besides, I don't need it; I want to be a truck driver."

Jason, of course, resisted by advancing all the usual arguments in favor of higher education. But when he realized the depths of Brian's unhappiness, he relented and did a most difficult thing: He relinquished his hopes. "Well, son," he said, "if that's what you want, go to it. I'll give you all the help I can."

I see in Jason a superb example of parental acceptance. Far from insisting on socioeconomic success for his children, he allows them to find their own level and, whatever that level, loves them dearly.

Aged eighteen, she was in her first year of university, living at home and bitterly resentful of the whole situation. In high school she had been a first-class student, but no longer. She had stopped working, and her marks were going from bad to worse. Around the house she was moody, irritable, uncooperative, hostile. Often there were quarrels, complete with shouting and screaming, followed by days of glacial silence.

"I'm at my wits' end," her mother confided one day to a close friend.

"Why don't you let her go?"

"I don't know—I guess I've just never thought of it."

But that same day she took her daughter aside. "I've been thinking about it," she said, "and I've come to the conclusion that, much as we'd love to keep you at home, it would be better if we helped you get settled in a place of your own. I know you'd like that."

Her daughter could scarcely believe what she had heard. "Do you mean it?"

"Of course I do, my dear. Now what can I do to help?"

Within two days, university abandoned, the girl had found an apartment, a friend to share the new quarters, and a job.

Relationships improved immediately and have gone on improving ever since.

It often happens. Parents say to their children, "Good-bye, go with our blessing," only to find those children closer than ever before.

Relinquishment, it seems, is often the means of recovery. Paradoxical? Yes, but true. We release someone, we say, "Go with my blessing," and, to our great surprise, we find that person, now more than ever, a loving presence in our lives.

Surrendering a child to life, even to a good life, can reduce us to tears. But surrendering a child to a life that is no life at all can break our hearts . . .

He was a big, gentle man
chief of police, he said
in another city and also
an elder in the church
He asked me
if I would please
go and see his daughter.

I found her
behind bars
a beautiful girl
but ravaged
by a drug habit
and life on the street
We talked
among other things
about family and home

I asked her
what she planned on doing
when she got out
She said, Oh, I guess
go back to my john.

I reported to her father
that, for the moment at least
I couldn't see much hope
Sorrowfully he said
Well, I guess
there's nothing we can do
but just let her go

. . .

And behold, the Cushite came; and the Cushite said, "Good tidings for my lord the king! For the Lord has delivered you this day from the power of all who rose up against you." The king said to the Cushite, "Is it well with the young man Absalom?" And the Cushite answered, "May the enemies of my lord the king, and all who rise up against you for evil, be like that young man." And the king was deeply moved, and went up to the chamber over the gate, and wept; and as he wept, he said, "O my son Absalom, my son, my son Absalom! Would I had died instead of you, O Absalom, my son, my son!"[4]

I know Harry and Jean, but I didn't know the circumstances of the death of their son. A mutual friend told me the story.

"Harry and Jean," he said, "arrived at the lake just as they were pulling young Scott's body out of the water. Imagine. Going away on a vacation, not a care in the world, and then being called back and seeing the recovery of your son's body.

"Scott's buddy, who had been part of the crowd on the night of the tragedy, was there too. He was on the dock, tears streaming down his face, while Harry, who had just lost a son—a son, remember—and who had far more reason to grieve had his arm around the kid's shoulder, trying to console him.

"I'll never forget the way Harry and Jean handled Scott's death," said my friend. "As long as I live, I'll remember their courage, their faith."

A precedent for parents: "For God so loved the world that he gave his only Son. . . ."[5]

Like most parents, Phyl and I have had occasional problems with our children. Serious problems. We have worried and pleaded, argued and wept, but have come finally to the place where all we could do was let go.

I see now that each such relinquishment is basically an affirmation, an act of faith, an expression of belief in the essential benevolence of life, belief that in the long, long run, as Julian of Norwich put it, "All shall be well and all shall be well and all manner of things shall be well."[6]

Your children are not your children.
They are the sons and daughters of Life's longing for
itself.
They come through you but not from you,
And though they are with you they belong not to you.

You may give them love but not your thoughts,
For they have their own thoughts.
You may house their bodies but not their souls,
For their souls dwell in the house of tomorrow, which
you cannot visit, not even in your dreams.
You may strive to be like them, but seek not to make
them like you.
For life goes not backward nor tarries with yesterday.
You are the bows from which your children as living
arrows are sent forth.
The archer sees the mark upon the path of the
infinite, and He bends you with His might that His
arrows may go swift and far.
Let your bending in the archer's hand be for gladness;
For even as He loves the arrow that flies, so He loves
also the bow that is stable.[7]

—Kahlil Gibran

3

IN PRAISE OF FOOLISHNESS

It was a long time ago. I laughed and gurgled and cooed. I howled and sobbed and wet my pants. I burped and drooled, smeared cereal all over my face, chewed at my toes. But now? Not so. I have matured. I have my dignity, my pride.

For instance, I slip on an icy sidewalk and land with a resounding thud on the flat of my back. What then? Do I take a couple of deep breaths? Do I check to see if I have broken an arm or a leg? No, the first thing I do, almost reflexively, is glance quickly up and down the street to see if anyone spotted my pratfall, my humiliation.

It is evident again and again—my concern for my image, my great reluctance to make a fool of myself.

Sad, isn't it? Once I was so freewheeling, so abandoned. But now all that has gone, or most of it. I am a model of propriety and decorum.

One summer when our children were still in their teens, we all went to see Robert Preston in *The Music Man*. I was humming "Seventy-Six Trombones" when we left the theater and still humming it when, several days later, we pulled into a parking lot in a strange town.

Stepping out of the car, I did something I could only have done in a strange place: I burst into joyous song and, à la Preston, started snaking my way through the lot, exhorting my brood to fall in line. "Come on, kids, join in!"

I remember being aware of their ambivalence. On the one hand, I sensed, they longed to cut loose, but on the other, it was hard for them to let themselves go.

(As it turned out, they compromised: They pitched in, but with a certain embarrassed restraint that said distinctly, "Thank God we're a thousand miles from home!")

I share in their ambivalence. I, too, am inhabited by the same conflicting *personae*—the Dionysian versus the Apollonian, the uninhibited clown versus the uptight executive in his three-piece suit.

Once in a while, as in the parking lot, the clown takes over. But mostly it is the executive who has the upper hand. He sees to it that I don't make a fool of myself in public places. God forbid.

> *If I Had My Life to Live Over*
>
> I'd like to make more mistakes next time. I'd relax. I would limber up. I would be sillier than I have been this trip. I would take fewer things seriously. I would take more chances. I would climb more mountains and swim more rivers. I would eat more ice cream and less beans. I would perhaps have more actual troubles, but I'd have fewer imaginary ones.
>
> You see, I'm one of those people who live sensibly and sanely hour after hour, day after day. Oh, I've had my moments, and if I had it to do over again I'd have more of them. In fact, I'd try to have nothing else. Just moments, one after another, instead of living so many years ahead of each day. I've been one of those persons who never goes anywhere without a thermometer, a hot water bottle, a raincoat and a parachute. If I had it to do over again, I would travel lighter than I have.
>
> If I had my life to live over, I would start barefoot earlier in the spring and stay that way later in the fall. I would go to more dances. I would ride more merry-go-rounds. I would pick more daisies.[1]
>
> —Nadine Stair (at age eighty-five)

"The great pleasure of a dog," said Samuel Butler, "is that you may make a fool of yourself with him and not only will he not scold you, but he will make a fool of himself too."

Also babies. We love them, among other reasons, because they call forth the child in us; they help us to let our hair down and behave like children ourselves.

It happens all the time: In the presence of a brand new human being, we become altogether different people. We lean over the crib, making the most absurd faces and gibbering absolute nonsense.

Infants give us that license, and we love them for it.

I think of grown-ups who have a great capacity for letting themselves go and who, in their spontaneity and abandon, are immensely endearing.

I think of Dick Sheppard, who fifty years ago was rector of St. Martin-in-the-Fields in the heart of London. Sheppard was a pacifist and a champion of the poor and oppressed. All through the depression St. Martin's helped the destitute, thousands upon thousands of them. On Sundays the church was filled to overflowing with people from every walk of life. Duchesses rubbed elbows with charwomen. Business moguls knelt alongside fishmongers.

A man of tremendous intensity, Sheppard died, burnt out, in middle age. But along with that dedication and drive, there was a joyousness, an enormous outgoing ebullience that endeared him to the whole city.

One day, so the story goes, a matron in a large hospital heard a huge commotion in one of the wards. She rushed in to see what on earth was happening, only to find Canon Sheppard—rector of St. Martin's, no less—lying flat on his back in the middle of the floor, waving one leg in the air to illustrate a hilarious story he was telling the patients, all of them convulsed with laughter and some of them, no doubt, in danger of literally popping their stitches.

I think of Keith, our eldest, who today can be a serious listener and tomorrow an out-and-out clown, leaving us limp with laughter.

We say, "Sing for us, Keith. 'Paper Roses!'" He usually obliges, even in the presence of total strangers, if not with "Paper Roses," then with "a little something I've added to my repertoire." It can be anything from rockabilly to the Lower Slobbovian national anthem. But whatever his choice, it is unfailingly *awful*. Excruciating. Deliberately off-key, dripping with sentiment and delivered in a stentorian bellow that would do him credit at a national hog callers' convention. We laugh until our sides hurt. Keith never cracks a smile.

> After breakfast we walked to the top of a very steep hill behind the house. When we arrived at the summit, Mr. Langton said, "Poor dear Dr. [Samuel] Johnson, when he came to this spot, turned back to look down the hill, and

> said he was determined 'to take a roll down.' When we understood what he meant to do, we endeavored to dissuade him; but he was resolute, saying, 'he had not had a roll for a long time'; and taking out of his lesser pockets whatever might be in them—keys, pencil, purse, or penknife—and laying himself parallel with the edge of the hill, he actually descended, turning himself over and over, till he came to the bottom."[2]
>
> —Henry Digby Beste

I can still see it, a picture of a bald, cadaverous old clergyman gloomily intoning the opening words of a service of worship: "I was glad when they said unto me, Let us go into the house of the Lord."

It is a pity that in so many instances the Church's mien belies its message.

I think of the time Mark Twain's wife attempted to launder her husband's language. She had expostulated over and over again, a hundred, a thousand times, but all to no avail. Samuel just kept right on swearing. Finally Livvy decided on shock tactics; she would show her husband how he really sounded by trotting out some bad language herself. It didn't work. Samuel burst out laughing. "My dear," he said, "you have the words all right, but you don't have the music!"

I often wish we had more of "the music" in church: the festivity (even the foolishness), the laughter, the joy.

Zen, we know, has a pronounced comedic element: the *koan*, the insoluble, apparently silly question; the master thumping his disciple over the head or kicking him in the seat of the pants (shades of Laurel and Hardy!).

It could be, though, that we are not so quick to recognize that the Christian faith, too, is in some ways downright ridiculous.

After all, what could be more nonsensical than to argue, along with St. Francis, that "it is in giving that we receive; it is in pardoning that we are pardoned; and it is in dying that we are born to eternal life"? Or to affirm that, in spite of the prevalence of disease, famine, and war, the whole of creation is pulsing with irresistible Love?

Looking at the saints, I see a strange, eccentric, even lunatic group . . .

Mohandas Gandhi, a spindly, bespectacled little man, clad only in a white *dhoti*, electing to oust the British colossus from India not with bullets and bombs but, eschewing all forms of violence, by digging in his heels and refusing to cooperate in any British enterprise. ("It's madness!")

Albert Schweitzer, forsaking a promising triple-threat career in favor of burying himself as a medical missionary in west-central Africa. ("He's out of his mind!")

Mother Teresa—who could, I suppose, have aimed at marriage to a Greek shipping magnate—immersing herself in the slums of Calcutta, there to spend her life in the service of the diseased, the destitute, the dying. ("What an idiotic idea!")

On the way home I met a friend who lived alone in a ramshackle caravan on a windy site overlooking the Atlantic, a tall imposing woman in her late sixties with a crown of grey hair piled on top of her head and tied with a velvet ribbon, wearing a thick ulster and waving a stout stick, singing at the top of her voice: "O all ye works of the Lord, bless ye the Lord, praise him and magnify him for ever! O all ye hills and oceans of the Lord, bless ye the Lord! La illah illa Alla! On mani padme hum!" Like a clipper ship, its sails bellied by the wind, she advanced and like many a full-rigger she had been battered by dreadful storms from every point of the human compass: deserted by two husbands, ruined by swindlers, her only child drowned by the carelessness of her best friend—she kept his ashes in her van—and now the victim of arthritis. "God bless!" she boomed, waving and rocking towards me. "You look done in. Why *do* you totter over to Morwenstow? You ought to know better. Let go, let go! Let go of people, passions, possessions, ideals, hopes, desires, treasures—everything! To live without sorrow or bitterness you must be able to do without, to give them all up. There's always more suffering than joy." And she shouted: "O all ye beasts and birds and fishes of the Lord, praise ye the Lord! And blessed be the great God Pan!" Rolling from side to side she whirled her stick and pushed past me, bawling: "Rejoice to-day with one accord, sing out with exultation. Rejoice and praise the mighty Lord whose arm has wrought salvation!" A gallant old lady, generous, brave, and rather goddess-like herself—a dethroned Juno, cast out of Olympus for some outrageous peccadillo that offended the other divinities, and hurled down to end her troubled and troubling existence on the wave-pounded Cornish coast. The last I saw of her—the last forever: she died soon afterwards—was her stick waving while her strong voice floated over hedgerows: "O all ye winds and waves and rainbows of the Lord, praise ye the Lord! . . ."[3]

—Adelaide Ross

It happened in my student days. I was speaking one summer afternoon in a backwoods community hall. It was a simple, almost primitive setting: no pulpit, only a table at the front of the hall; no pews, just several rows of rough, backless benches; no organ, in fact not even a piano.

I talked that day about generosity. In the course of the sermon there was a funny story, one I still remember with a certain embarrassment—it certainly didn't come under the heading of high-class humor. But for some reason it struck a responsive chord in Mrs. Fisher, a cheerful soul sitting in the front row. She began heaving with suppressed laughter. Others noticed her and began heaving too. I maintained my composure as long as I could, but finally burst out laughing myself. At that point everyone exploded, and within seconds we were, almost literally, rolling in the aisles—clutching our sides, tears streaming down our faces, all of us doubled up in helpless mirth.

It was how the service ended. No closing hymn. No benediction. No organ postlude. Just great rollicking gales of laughter.

We left feeling a little irreverent and foolish. But as I look back on the incident, I am sure that the Eternal shared our joy.

God . . . *plays*. That is the point missed by so much of our religiosity. We contemplate his "works" and judge them a fitting environment for human business. How prosaic! How dull! The works of God are a cosmic shout, a dance of planets, and a theater for *glory*. God did not create the universe out of need; he made it "just for fun." It is rather like what is meant when we speak of the play of imagination or the creative play of genius. When an artist engages in that creative talent which is his special "thing," he comes up with something; he produces a work which reflects his own pleasure, a kind of plaything. Others may find it pleasant or not, beautiful or not; he doesn't really care. So God created a universe, and his work reflects his own creative being, the free play of his choice. After he made it—so the old story goes—he "saw that it was good" and began to busy himself with enjoying it. So also, we are told, did those beings who witnessed the original creation: "the morning stars sang together and all the sons of God shouted for joy."[4]

—Joseph C. McLelland

It was back in the late forties. Working in wilderness country on the north shore of Lake Superior, I was one of a crew that included two brothers. When I first saw those two, I remember, I felt a strange unease, and that disquieting feeling, that fear, was with me all summer. Physically, they were a powerful duo—stocky, barrel-chested, muscular men with a primitive, almost Neanderthal quality.

I never talked with them; nor, I believe, did anyone else, for they didn't invite conversation. In fact, they seldom spoke even between themselves. A silent, withdrawn pair, they seemed to be harboring something alien and ugly, something downright menacing.

Among the rest of us there were the usual antics and jokes, the clowning and horseplay, but the brothers never entered into our lighthearted shenanigans. All summer long they remained aloof, a cold and forbidding pair.

Evil, like those two, is unsmiling and grim. Evil doesn't frolic, doesn't let its hair down and behave in some idiotic, abandoned fashion. Evil is stiff and unbending, formal and cold.

Love, on the other hand, is loose and uninhibited. Love is comic and antic, a natural clown. Love knows how to laugh, to play, to let itself go.

Consider sex, love's most intimate expression. Sex, we know, is a serious business, bound up with the procreation of the species, a whole body of moral implications and, often, sighs too deep for words. But at the same time, let's face it, sex has a lighter side. At its best, certainly, sex is both serious and nonserious; sex is at times playful and antic, frivolous and extravagant. For animals, no, not really, but for humans, yes, sex is *fun.*

> We must not be totally serious about Venus. Indeed we can't be totally serious without doing violence to our humanity. It is not for nothing that every language and literature in the world is full of jokes about sex. Many of them may be dull or disgusting and nearly all of them are old. But we must insist that they embody an attitude to Venus which in the long run endangers the Christian life far less than a reverential gravity. We must not attempt to find an absolute in the flesh. Banish play and laughter from the bed of love and you may let in a false goddess. She will be even falser than the Aphrodite of the Greeks; for they, even while they worshipped her, knew that she was "laughter-loving." The mass of the people are perfectly right in their conviction that Venus is partly a comic spirit. We are under no obligation at all to sing all our love-duets in the throbbing, world-without-end, heart-breaking manner of Tristan and Isolde; let us often sing like Papageno and Papagena instead.[5]
>
> —C. S. Lewis

Odd, perhaps, but true: The clowns in our midst and the saints in our pantheon of immortals have much in common.

After all, the clowns, too, are behaving with a certain crazy extravagance. True, they aren't discarding quite the same things as the saints—wealth, for one, and status and power. But they, too, are squanderers, gladly saying good-bye to self-importance, to dignity, to pride—items that to most people are of great value.

Another point of similarity: The clowns also are instruments of joy. Like their colleagues the saints, but in their own way, they gladden the hearts of their neighbors. They make the world a brighter and better place—and in the process are themselves blessed.

> God, but I want madness!
> I want to tremble,
> to be shaken,
> to yield to pulsation,

to surrender to the rhythm of music and sea,
to the seasons of ebb and flow,
to the tidal surge of love.

I am tired of being
hard,
tight,
controlled,
tensed against the invasion of novelty,
afraid of softness.
I am tired of
directing my world,
making,
doing,
shaping.
Tension is ecstasy in chains.
The muscles are tightened to prevent trembling.
Nerves strain to prevent trust, hope, relaxation.

Surrendering,
giving in to the involuntary is:
madness (idiots tremble),
ecstasy (being out of my skin, who am I?),
bliss (love is coming together and parting),
grace (dancing with the whole spirit).

Surrendering,
giving in to the involuntary is:
insanity (which voices are mine?),
terror (now, who am I?),
torture (aliens are fighting in my brain),
being possessed (by a god or a demon, or both).

Which:
madness or insanity,
trembling or being afraid,
enthusiasm or possession?
The path is narrow to the right madness.
Be wary of trembling in the wrong places!
The demons often disguise themselves as gods.
And vice versa.

* * *

Surrender is a risk no sane man may take.
Sanity never surrendered is a burden no man may carry.

God, give me madness
that does not destroy
wisdom,
responsibility,
love.[6]

—Sam Keen

4

THE FRUGALITY PHENOMENON

We bought the island twenty years ago for a mere $500. It seemed a lot of money at the time. In fact, it was far more than we had. We had to borrow the money from a bank. Still, it was a trifling sum to pay for what we received in return—four acres of tall-pined serenity in an inland sea of dazzling beauty.

Our first boat, necessary for commuting to and from "the mainland," was simplicity itself—a fourteen-foot all-aluminum craft, wide open, with an old 7.5 horsepower outboard. It served us faithfully and well. But then I began getting some grandiose notions. How nice it would be, I thought, to have a boat with more power and speed. Also a convertible top to keep us dry in foul weather. Also cushioned seats, electric start, and all the amenities.

I ended up buying, secondhand, a sleek fiberglass runabout that turned out to be an absolute disaster. It balked at starting and, finally underway, wallowed and plowed like an exhausted moose. Heading into even a slight chop, it pounded unmercifully and, several times, sprang leaks of major proportions. One morning, I remember, I looked out and saw the boat awash almost to the gunwales, all, it developed, because of a crack in the hull, a six-inch split we had unknowingly incurred the previous evening.

After a single season I sold the glamorous little runabout and bought a boat much like the one I'd had originally, a plain, straightforward craft without all the gadgets and frills. We have had clear sailing ever since.

It was not the only time I have bought some sophisticated piece of equipment that proved to be a king-sized aggravation. As a matter of fact, it has happened so often that I have long since reached the point where I am in total agreement with E. F. Schumacher's emphasis on "intermediate technology."

High-tech stuff, it seems, is often totally inimical to peace of mind.

I had a dream: I returned home after a brief absence and found that Phyl had gone ahead, solo, and bought a huge old mansion in a state of appalling dilapidation. "I got it for a song," she said. But what a mess! Inside were dozens of rooms and corridors, all of them with plaster fallen from the ceilings, paper peeling off the walls, and flooring cracked and stained. Outside it was just as bad—acres of grounds that, after years of neglect, had become almost a jungle. It was a place that spelled not only years of hard labor but also sums of money I didn't begin to have. I was beside myself with dismay, until eventually I wakened—in our snug little home—with an immense sigh of relief.

No, I don't envy people who live in palatial homes. I remember Dorothy, who was virtually a prisoner, afraid to leave her estate lest "thieves break in and steal" her silver, her paintings, her antiques.

But then we have all had some experience of "the tyranny of things." We know from personal experience that the things we possess can, and often do, possess us; they dominate our lives, dictate our coming and going, drive us to distraction.

A friend put it succinctly, if somewhat inelegantly, when he growled, "Ownership is a pain in the ass."

In her autobiography, *All I Want Is Everything*, Marion Preminger recalls a visit with Albert Schweitzer: "Once in Africa, when the Governor General was expected to come to the hospital on a visit, I dared to say to Dr. Schweitzer, 'Herr Professor, this black tie you are wearing is already very much worn.' He said, 'I can't imagine why. I have had it only 18 years and I have worn it only to christenings and funerals.'

"'Eighteen years!' I exclaimed. 'Don't you have another, a second, tie?'

"'Fortunately not,' he said. 'My father had two, and I remember how they were always looking for the better tie.'"

Mother Teresa is someone else with a meager wardrobe. In fact, wherever she goes, be it to receive a Nobel prize or to clean the convent toilets, her dress is always the same: a blue-edged coarse white cotton *sari*, the garment of peasant women throughout India.

Mohandas Gandhi left an estate that, apart from a few items of clothing, consisted of only a pair of spectacles, a pocket watch, an inkwell and paper-knife, two pairs of sandals, a couple of feeding bowls with two wooden spoons, a small image of the three wise monkeys, a rosary, a hymn book, and a copy of the *Bhagavad Gita*.

Albert Einstein was a familiar figure in Princeton, trudging around with his long white hair uncombed and his dress a sartorial shambles: a shabby old pullover and overcoat, a pair of vintage corduroy trousers, and shoes without socks. ("I don't like to trouble my wife with a lot of washing.") A company once sent Einstein a check, a handsome sum, in return for his consulting services. Typically, he used the check for a bookmark, then lost the book.

Jean Vanier, son of a former Governor General of Canada, is a Roman Catholic layman who in 1964 moved into a dilapidated old house in Trosly, France, to share his life with two retarded men. Since then, *L'Arche* (The Ark) communities, in which the normal and the retarded live a common life, have opened on four continents. I once went to hear Vanier speak. Like most of the others, I went dressed for the occasion, but not so Vanier himself. He appeared, his face luminous with love, in an old tweed coat, baggy trousers, and shoes cracked with age. I felt shamed by his simplicity and sheer goodness.

I can see only one explanation for the saints' remarkable indifference to material wealth and a multiplicity of possessions: So inwardly secure are these people, so wealthy in their interior lives, that they simply don't need all the accoutrements—the extensive wardrobes and expensive cars, the gadgets and trinkets—that so often serve to buttress our fragile egos.

> Socrates was wont to say, They are most happy and nearest the gods that needed nothing. And coming once up into the Exchange at Athens, where they that traded asked him, What will you buy? What do you lack?, after he had gravely walked up into the middle, spreading forth his hands and turning about: Good gods, said he, who would have thought there were so many things in the world which I do not want! And so left the place under the reproach of Nature. He was wont to say: That Happiness

> consisted not in having many, but in needing the fewest things: for the gods needed nothing at all, and they were most like them who least needed.[1]
>
> —Thomas Traherne

I suspect that the timeless appeal of the Eden story lies largely in the idyllic simplicity of which it speaks. No mortgage payments and difficult people. No pollution or crime, poverty or disease. No nuclear bombs. Just two people in a garden.

As a child, I remember, I read *Robinson Crusoe.* I had no particular problems at the time; life was good. But even so, I envied Crusoe. Deeply. I can remember the wistfulness, the longing almost, for some lonely, beautiful place where, with no music lessons and homework assignments, no tapioca pudding and compulsory bedtime, I would have nothing to do all day long but build ship models, gorge myself on tropical fruits, and cavort in the surf.

I wonder when that longing for Eden arises. Is it something that goes back to early childhood? Or does it go back even further than that? Is it something we are born with, something native to the human heart? Possibly so.

I am sure, though, that the longing is intensified by the pressures under which we live. In a simple, agrarian society, I would guess, our forefathers had less need of Eden simply because there was more of Eden in their everyday lives. It was there in a more fundamental way of life; it was there in the forests and fields, in the valleys and lakes, the meadows and hills.

But today? A different scene. Crowded expressways and high-decibel rock. Vice, terrorism, and dwindling resources. A population explosion, long lines at the unemployment office, and, overhanging everything, the threat of nuclear annihilation.

Given such a grim and stressful world, is it any wonder that people everywhere are aching for a lost innocence, a way of life that spells simplicity and peace?

> One learns first of all in beach living the art of shedding; how little one can get along with, not how much. Physical shedding to begin with, which then mysteriously spreads into other fields. Clothes, first. Of course, one needs less

in the sun. But one needs less anyway, one finds suddenly. One does not need a closet-full. And what a relief it is! Less taking up and down of hems, less mending, and—best of all—less worry about what to wear. One finds one is shedding not only clothes—but vanity.

Next, shelter. One does not need the airtight shelter one has in winter in the North. Here I live in a bare sea-shell of a cottage. No heat, no telephone, no plumbing to speak of, no hot water, a two-burner oil stove, no gadgets to go wrong. No rugs. There were some, but I rolled them up the first day; it is easier to sweep the sand off a bare floor. But I find I don't bustle about with unnecessary sweeping and cleaning here. I am no longer aware of the dust. I have shed my Puritan conscience about absolute tidiness and cleanliness. Is it possible that, too, is a material burden? No curtains. I do not need them for privacy; the pines around my house are enough protection. I want the windows open all the time, and I don't want to worry about rain. I begin to shed my Martha-like anxiety about many things. Washable slipcovers, faded and old—I hardly see them; I don't worry about the impression they make on other people. I am shedding pride. As little furniture as possible; I shall not need much. I shall ask into my shell only those friends with whom I can be completely honest. I find I am shedding hypocrisy in human relationships. What a rest that will be! The most exhausting thing in life, I have discovered, is being insincere. That is why so much of social life is exhausting; one is wearing a mask. I have shed my mask. . . .

Is it not rather ugly, one may ask? One collects material possessions not only for security, comfort or vanity, but for beauty as well. Is your sea-shell house not ugly and bare? No, it is beautiful, my house. It is bare, of course, but the wind, the sun, the smell of the pines blow through its bareness. The unfinished beams in the roof are veiled by cobwebs. They are lovely, I think, gazing up at them with new eyes; they soften the hard lines of the rafters as grey hairs soften the lines in a middle-aged face. I no longer pull out grey hairs or sweep down cobwebs. As for the walls, it is true they looked forbidding at first. I felt

> cramped and enclosed by their blank faces. I wanted to knock holes in them, to give them another dimension with pictures or windows. So I dragged home from the beach grey arms of driftwood, worn satin smooth by wind and sand. I gathered trailing green vines with floppy red-tipped leaves. I picked up the whitened skeletons of conchshells, with their curious hollowed-out shapes faintly reminiscent of abstract sculpture. With these tacked to walls and propped up in corners, I am satisfied.[2]
>
> —Anne Morrow Lindbergh

Industrial psychologists call it the "antique store syndrome." ("I've got to get out of the rat race and open up a little antique store somewhere.") It is a familiar pattern; one sees it again and again. Fed up with the pressures of urban society and the overwhelming complexity of their crowded lives, people go back to the land or otherwise opt for a simpler lifestyle.

A Ph.D. in agriculture leaves a good job with the government in favor of small-scale farming. At the same time his wife opens up a health-food store. It turns out to be a winning combination, with the couple using the produce from the farm, including the large quantity of bread they bake each week, not only to feed their family but also to stock the store.

A teacher in a public school system abruptly quits his job. His new career? A little of everything: plumbing, carpentry, wallpapering, cleaning apartments. His income drops sharply, and his life is stripped of many of its former frills. But there are substantial compensations, including time for the pursuit of a long-standing interest in painting.

A Baltimore man, owner and operator of a trucking business, finds his work profitable but far from satisfying. Finally, fed up with it all, he takes a decisive step: He sells out. What he wants to do now, he says, is somehow combine two interests he has had for a long time—woodworking and children. He ends up, an eminently happy man, crafting superb—and highly saleable—wooden toys in a small shop in Pennsylvania.

A successful but dissatisfied young interior designer leaves the chic, glittering world of his wealthy clientele for something entirely different. He buys a thrift store in Greenwich Village and moves from an elegant apartment in the Dakota, complete with houseman, to "a very crummy" place in the vicinity of his store. "I don't make any money now," he says, "and it will be years before I do, but even with the problems, I'm much happier."

An account executive with an impressive income drops out of corporate life at age forty-five. His intention is to earn a living, however basic, by devoting full time to wildlife sculpture, a hobby he has enjoyed for years. Initially, he spends sixteen hours a day, week in and week out, down in his basement workshop. Success soon comes. Fifteen months after beginning, he sells twenty-two pieces for $35,000 and is commissioned to sculpt figures worth $25,000 more. He goes on to see his works displayed in several of the continent's major galleries and museums, including the Smithsonian Institution.

I know people who, in their pursuit of simplicity, have radically altered the shape of their lives. But I know even more people who go to the office each day, mow the lawn on Saturday afternoons and, on Sunday mornings, sing in the church choir, yet who, in their very ordinariness, lead lives of extraordinary simplicity.

I think of Gerry and Shirley, friends of long standing. Gerry is a good and gifted man, one whose career has been spent largely in academic circles. Shirley is a highly competent secretary and one of the warmest, most genuine people I know. Not of necessity, then, but by choice, these two are absolutely committed to a simple lifestyle. A minimal wardrobe. No car, for a time. Infrequent haircuts. Plain, basic foods. Inexpensive vacations.

At one time Gerry and Shirley would have been oddballs, freaks. But not now. Today thousands upon thousands of people have quietly foresworn "conspicuous consumption" and are creating, right where they are, their own equivalents to Walden Pond.

> During the decade of the 1970s, a quiet revolution has been stirring at the grass roots level of virtually every Western industrial nation. People from all walks of life have been experimenting with alternative ways of living that touch the world more lightly, more gently, more compassionately. In their own unique manner, teachers, factory workers, lawyers, carpenters, farmers, students, and many more have been exploring alternative ways of

living. For the most part, their experiments in living have been modest and have not attracted much attention: A city dweller plants his first intensive garden; a suburban family insulates its home, begins to recycle bottles, cans, and paper, and begins to shift its diet away from meat and highly processed foods; a student becomes a member of a consumer-owned food store; a lawyer learns carpentry as an alternative profession; a family decides not to buy a new car or a new television or a new dishwasher; and so on.

The majority of people who are undertaking these diverse and seemingly small experiments in simple living are not so much "purists" as they are "pioneers." They are persons who stand with a foot in two worlds—with one foot in an unraveling industrial civilization and another foot in a newly arising post-industrial civilization. These are the "in-betweeners"—people who are bridging two worlds and making the transition from one dominant way of living to another. Their way of living is an amalgam, a blending of the old and new into a more workable and meaningful alternative to the deteriorating status quo.[3]

—Duane Elgin

It was a grey, drizzly September afternoon, and I was standing, waiting for Phyl, under one of the canopies of a large downtown department store. People were streaming by, hundreds of them and nearly all of them oblivious to my presence. Normally I would have paid them no more attention than they paid me. But this time, whatever the reason, I found myself looking deeply into their faces, actually *seeing* them. It was a haunting experience—so much so, in fact, that I can still see some of those faces . . .

A Chinese girl of about twenty and wearing a grey, belted raincoat. Tall and slim with long ebony hair, she would have been attractive if her face hadn't been creased in an angry scowl, her beauty obscured by her mood.

A middle-aged businessman hurrying by, briefcase in hand, with anxiety and strain written all over his face. Signs of prosperity? Definitely. But "the peace that passeth understanding"? None of it.

A rangy, red-headed boy in his late teens or early twenties, clad in a tweed jacket and a pair of jeans. With an open sunburned face, he was obviously someone who earned his living outdoors. In construction, perhaps, or farming. But what I noticed especially was the distant, worried look. He seemed preoccupied, troubled by something miles away.

A young woman with hands stuffed into her coat pockets, her eyelids puffy and red, her eyes brimming with tears. She was one of the few people who noticed me. When she saw me looking at her, she hurried by, her face averted, embarrassed because a stranger had witnessed her grief.

Atypical, these people? By no means. I saw dozens like them, people of all ages who seemed driven and tense, pressured and grim. Joy, in fact, seemed almost totally absent. One person in ten, perhaps, was clearly happy, but no more.

Strange, isn't it? Here we are, one of the most affluent societies on earth but still aching and bedeviled, still broken and unfulfilled. Our affluence, it seems, has brought us little joy.

Which perhaps helps to explain the swing to simplicity: We have tried affluence and found it wanting.

> What the world lives by at the moment just will not do. Nor will it; nor do very many people suppose any longer that it will. Countries like ours are full of people who have all the material comforts they desire, yet lead lives of quiet (and at times noisy) desperation, understanding nothing but the fact that there is a hole inside them and that however much food and drink they pour into it, however many motorcars and television sets they stuff it with, however many well-balanced children and loyal friends they parade around the edges of it . . . it *aches.*[4]
>
> —Bernard Levin

Another, and I think even more compelling, argument for "plain living" is the desperate situation of the human race.

In Calcutta alone, 600,000 people, dressed in rags, are perpetually homeless—picking up scraps of food wherever they can, cooking over little open fires, defecating in the gutters, sleeping in culverts, doorways, packing crates, and dying in the night, their corpses hauled away by truck in the early hours of the morning.

Throughout the world people are dying of starvation at the rate of ten thousand per day, over four hundred per hour. Children are the most lamentable victims, with fifteen million under the age of five dying each year of sheer hunger. Every two seconds, somewhere, a child falls prey to starvation.

In North America? An entirely different scene. Garbage cans overflow with good food. Surplus grain rots in storage bins while farmers await higher prices. Pets are better fed here than children are in Third World countries. Gross obesity is a problem for a multitude of people. Dieting is a national obsession. "A million hogs in Indiana have superior housing to a billion humans on this planet."[5]

Richard J. Foster points out, "America has 6 percent of the world's population and consumes 33 percent of the world's resources. If the rest of the world were to attempt to live on our level of consumption it is projected that all known world resources of petroleum, tin, zinc, natural gas, lead, copper, tungsten, gold and mercury would be exhausted in ten years. Put simply, the earth cannot afford our lifestyle. No, the answer is clear: we must cut back our standard of living if there is ever to be anything approaching a just distribution of the world's resources."[6]

Foster is right: Both the heart and the mind, both compassion and commonsense now dictate a more frugal way of life. In view of the crying need of the human race and the alarming depletion of nonrenewable resources, we have no other humane and sensible option; we simply must reduce our standard of living.

A poster put it in a nutshell: "Live simply so that others may simply live."

5

"I'M UNCOMFORTABLE AROUND GODS"

I study the long list of notices in the Personals and I am saddened by what I see: women and men, black people and white people, the young and the old, heterosexual and gay, people of every description, some serious and some flip, but all of them appealing—no, crying—for lovers and friends, all of them so clearly and painfully *lonely.*

But it is not only the Personals: pet shops and massage parlors, cults, communes, and computer dating services, est, Esalen, church groups and Golden Age clubs, singles bars, self-help books and a succession of one-night stands, plus alcoholic oblivion and the deep sleep of death, each offering an antidote to our society's pandemic *loneliness.*

In Hamburg, Germany in 1975, 73-year-old August Heise was found on the floor of his apartment, a television program guide clutched in his lifeless hands. He had been dead six months. No one knew until a niece happened to drop by. Though at least 10 neighbors passed his door daily, none had bothered to knock. And bill collectors, who ordinarily might discover when something is wrong, never came—Heise's bank automatically took care of his rent and utility payments.[1]

I am convinced that one of the chief, though least recognized, causes of loneliness is phoniness, artificiality.

Leslie Weatherhead used a memorable phrase when he spoke of "the loneliness of pretense." It is a phrase that points to a familiar pattern, certainly in my own life . . .

I present myself as someone other than I am and in so doing effectively obscure my true self. People are unable to see that self, unable to get a fix on who and what I am, unable to find anything *real* to which they can relate. The result? They turn to someone else, someone less puzzling and more genuine, and I am left out in the cold.

All too often, I am afraid, I present only my superior self. I give (or try to give) the impression that I am never bewildered, frightened, ashamed; I never fail on the job, never quarrel with my wife or agonize over my children; I never "cry me a river," never do battle with demons, never succumb to despair.

In short, I present only one side of my being. I fail to disclose the negative side, the "shadow side" of which Jung spoke so perceptively.

I lie. I lie in the sense that I don't tell the whole truth. And what happens? I invite resentment and envy; I intimidate and alienate the very people I hope to attract, people who, if they only knew it, are just like myself but who are (understandably) convinced that they and I have nothing in common, certainly nothing on which to build friendship and love.

I can empathize with the woman who wrote a popular columnist, complaining that she was fed up, in fact infuriated by the general run of mimeographed Christmas letters. Most of them, she said, are so smug, if not downright boastful, that they are enough to turn one's stomach.

Look, she said, at a typical letter: hubby has been given a huge promotion by the bank ("We celebrated by going to Europe and buying a Mercedes") and appointed to several important civic offices; she herself (the banker's wife and the writer of the Christmas epistle) has just completed a term as president of the Junior League but is still involved—in leadership roles, of course—in an awesome array of church and community groups; as for the children, they, too, are doing superbly—Junior is off to Harvard and his younger sister, no less than he, seems headed for the top.

What she would like to do sometime, said the complainant, is write a letter "telling it like it is"—something like this: My husband is out of work and drinking like a fish, our kids are giving us no end of trouble, and, after an extended visit from my mother-in-law, I myself "am back in therapy."

I am in total agreement with the woman who wanted no more self-adulation; I, too, find it hard to relate to the authors of the glittering success stories. But the people who share their struggles and woes? Ah, how I relate to them!

A priest. He impressed me as being one of the saintliest people I had ever known. But much as I admired him, I never felt close to him, never felt that we shared the same world. In fact, he functioned on such a superior plane—or so it seemed—that whenever I was with him, I felt a little grubby and ashamed.

(A year or so after our paths diverged, as it turned out, my clerical acquaintance was found guilty of criminal misbehavior, his priesthood terminated.)

I recognize, though, that often I have had precisely the same effect on people myself: my "goodness," my rectitude has made them uncomfortable.

What we need, it seems, is not the goodness that is stiff, cold, punctilious, correct, the goodness that intimidates and alienates its neighbors. What we need, rather, is the *karos* of which the Greeks spoke, the goodness that is warm, attractive, endearing, the goodness that causes its neighbors to glow with joy.

> When Bruce said he had trouble getting along with his mother, I liked him better. I like a man with faults, especially when he knows it. To err is human—I'm uncomfortable around gods.[2]
>
> —Hugh Prather

Odd that it should come to me now. But then so much of writing is like that—insights and memories, small, touching gifts that come out of the blue . . .

To be more specific, I remember Fred Weir, who taught me Latin in high school, the best teacher I ever had; I remember him telling us one day about the origin of the word *sincere*.

"Long ago," he said, "there were stonemasons and sculptors—shoddy workers, unscrupulous people—who used to gull the public by filling in the cracks and gouges in their work with wax. Sooner or later, of course, the wax fell out and people were furious.

"Honest artisans, however, used to advertise their work as *sine cera*—without wax."

Sincere: "Free from pretence or deceit, the same in reality as in appearance or seeming or profession, not assumed or put on, genuine, honest, frank."[3]

> Be true! Be true! Be true! Show freely to the world if not your worst, yet some trait whereby the worst may be inferred.[4]
>
> —Nathaniel Hawthorne

If I were ever to write a popularity manual (God forbid), I wouldn't talk about dress, grooming, etiquette, and so on. I would talk about self-disclosure, about the importance of being candid, natural, unpretentious. Or, in a word, sincere.

People come to mind: Jack and Evelyn and Tony and Pat, to name only a few. People who consistently present themselves as they are, "warts and all." People who, in their openness, are marvelously endearing.

A Canadian cabinet minister I sat beside at a luncheon. In an extraordinarily candid address, he admitted to yielding to political pressure and doing something patently wrong. "The fact is," he said, "that I weakened. I've regretted it ever since." I was deeply impressed by his honesty.

A friend who shared in a letter some of the difficulties he and his wife had been having with one of their children. I was drawn to him as never before, not only because he had shared his pain but also because I could identify with him: Phyl and I had been having precisely the same problem with one of our own children.

A friend who one day confessed to an unfortunate premarital history. "I don't know what you'll think of me," she concluded. "But I don't like being a phoney. I had to tell you." Think of her? I had never appreciated her more.

Self-disclosure, I have come to see, is a powerful force. It can thaw people out, draw them out, bring them together. It can convert massive interpersonal barriers into the bridges by which we move from heart to heart and rejoice in our common humanity.

> At 75, Truman was asked by a Missouri boy: "Mr. Truman, was you popular when you was a boy?"
>
> "Why, no," Truman answered. "I was never popular. The popular boys were the ones who were good at games

and had big, tight fists. I was never like that. Without my glasses I was blind as a bat, and to tell the truth, I was kind of a sissy. If there was any danger of getting into a fight, I always ran. I guess that's why I'm here today."[5]

—Leo Rosten

He never put on airs.[6]

—Bess Truman

It seems to be widely recognized that self-disclosure is a sign of self-confidence, that only the inwardly secure allow themselves to be open and vulnerable.

I wonder, though, if we are so quick to recognize that self-disclosure is also a sign of our confidence in others. Which is to say, when I expose my failure, my inadequacy, my need, I trust; I trust my listener not to condemn and reject but to understand and accept.

It comes down to this: Self-disclosure is an act of faith that, like any act of true faith, entails certain risks and at the same time offers substantial rewards.

I begin to think, after a year in prison, that the only thing that really matters on earth is that a man should escape from his isolation. That he should be able to drop *all* screens and defenses. That people should not be afraid of each other. That human beings should cherish the human life in each other, and love all things human. That is the lesson I get out of prison. Love one another. You can't just start doing it, as the bogus Christians think, by repeating the words aloud; the word deputises much too readily for the fact. You have to do precisely what Christ said—throw away all your defences, your goods, your little self-loves which you have deified, and make yourself utterly vulnerable, as Christ was to Judas and Pilate. You have to expose your soul, make the great gesture of trust; you have to cast *all* your bread upon the waters. To be strong, admit your weakness, to be safe, accept all danger. To lose all fear, take off your armour and throw away your sword. . . . Deny this through fear, and you deny your life. . . .

I suppose there are some prisons which can never be broken open—personal prisons, which were first built for protection, but which keep the besieged as fast inside as the besiegers outside—and what if there was *no* enemy, after all? To carry the useless carapace of doubt up to the grave, like a snail in its shell.

But for each man there must be . . . a key to his prison-door. When and if the future turns that key, they will come at last into the sunshine. Because there is no sunshine unless there is trust and love.

And that, not intellect and knowledge, is what we turn to in each other. When people do not find my opinion worth their respect, I know it is not because I lack intelligence or knowledge, but because I am shut away from them in a distrust which forces similar distrust on them. And when, as happens more and more here, people bring their problems to me, I know that that is no compliment to my learning. It is better than that. It is a recognition on their part that I am *free* to listen to them, that I am open to them, that I am in some sort a free man. . . .

Do not make tremendous efforts; true escape is not a flight, a running away. It is only when the prison walls drop, drop away from around you, that you truly escape.[7]

6

THE COURAGE TO LOVE

On the one hand . . .

Senior minister to one of the largest congregations in the nation, he was a distinguished figure and, more important, kindness personified.

We belonged to the same presbytery, he and I, but whereas I was only a novice in ministry, he was a giant, towering far above me in terms of influence and renown.

A few of our presbytery meetings, I remember, degenerated into verbal brawls. Charges and counter-charges flew back and forth across the floor. People, myself included, were furious. He, though, never got involved in all that acrimony. He remained apart from it, above it.

I remember, too, how, as those unfortunate meetings drew to a close, it was always he who said the soothing, healing thing. It was always he who found something to appreciate, something to praise.

He was one of the kindest, most appreciative men I have ever known. His life was a benediction.

On the other hand . . .

He is a successful businessman, active in civic affairs and a generous donor to charitable causes. He is a faithful husband and a good father. But perhaps because he was raised in a thankless home, he has great difficulty in voicing simple gratitude. He expresses appreciation, if at all, only through odd strangulated monosyllables.

I know others like him, people who suffer from emotional constipation.

It was a summer afternoon. I was working out in the back yard. Watching were my son and his friend Peter. At one point in the proceedings I asked Keith to pass me a hammer. He did so and I thanked him.

Afterward, amazed, Peter asked him, "Does he do that often?"

"Do what?"

"Say thank you."

"Sure, doesn't your dad?"

"No. Never."

It was my son's turn to be amazed—so much so, in fact, that he related the conversation over the supper table. "Can you believe it? Peter's dad has never thanked him for a single thing in his whole life. Not once."

In the twenty years that have passed since then, the children in that family have undergone a miserable time: drug addiction, divorce, mental illness, and death.

I wonder how much of their pain can be attributed to the cold, thankless environment in which they were raised.

> No parent should be afraid to use praise. John Newton used to say: "I knew that my father loved me, but he seemed unwilling that I should know it."
>
> Poor Mary Lamb, Charles' sister, had life punctuated by periods of madness. She knew when the times were coming, and she and Charles used to go hand in hand to the asylum where for a time she had to be confined. When she was young, she used to say despairingly: "Why is it that I never seem to be able to do anything to please my mother?" And maybe a parent's severity was responsible for much.[1]
>
> —William Barclay

L. P. Jacks once observed that when it comes to criticism, we are highly articulate; our words come out in a torrent that can go on and on. But, he said, when it comes to appreciation and affection, we are strangely tongue-tied; we find it hard to say "Thank you" and harder still to say "I love you."

I wonder why. Is this just another indication of the built-in bias that theologians have labeled original sin?

Or is it that appreciation is a function of novelty and, along with novelty, has a limited life span? Is it that time causes love to be taken for granted, that time tends to blind us to grace?

If so, that too may be evidence of our essential—and unfortunate—predilection for the worse rather than the better.

> My friend Art Sueltz [tells] . . . about the seven stages of a cold in the life of a young married couple. The first year the husband says, "Sugar, I'm worried about my little baby girl. You've got a bad sniffle. I want to put you in the hospital for a complete checkup. I know the food is lousy, but I've arranged for your meals to be sent up from Rossini's. It's all arranged."
>
> The second year: "Listen, honey, I don't like the sound of that cough. I've called Dr. Miller and he's going to rush right over. Now will you go to bed like a good girl just for me, please?"
>
> Third year: "Maybe you'd better lie down, honey. Nothing like a little rest if you're feeling bad. I'll bring you something to eat. Have we got any soup in the house?"
>
> Fourth year: "Look, dear. Be sensible. After you've fed the kids and washed the dishes you'd better hit the sack."
>
> Fifth year: "Why don't you take a couple of aspirin?"
>
> Sixth year: "If you'd just gargle or something instead of sitting around barking like a seal."
>
> Seventh year: "For heaven's sake stop sneezing. What are you trying to do, give me pneumonia?"[2]
>
> —Bruce Larson

I am amazed by men who absently eat a meal that has taken hours to prepare, then get up from the table without even a word of thanks to their wives, much less an offer to help with the dishes, and slouch off to read the paper, watch TV, and fall asleep.

> He put coffee
> In the cup
> He put cream
> In the cup of coffee
> He put sugar
> In the coffee cup
> With the little spoon
> He stirred it up
> He tried a sip
> He put back the cup

He never spoke
He lit
A cigarette
He made rings
Of the smoke
He put the ashes
In the ash tray
Without talking to me
Without taking note
He stood up
He put
His hat on his head
He put on his raincoat
And he went away
Without a word
Without a glance aside
And me I laid
My head in my hand
And I cried.[3]

—Jacques Prévert

I went out to the island in late May, weary in body and depleted in spirit. For three weeks I was there, completely alone. Later in the season there would be cottagers on other islands and boats passing by, but at that time of year the nearest person was miles away. Only the gulls were there for company, and a few animals—beaver and deer, a fox at the edge of some woods, and a solitary porcupine swimming across the mouth of a nearby bay.

I did not miss the usual amenities, the stereo system and central heating, the refrigeration and running water, hot and cold. But what I did miss, acutely and increasingly, was people. I missed family and friends. I missed their love.

I have speculated on what would have happened if those three weeks of isolation had been extended to three months, three years, three decades. In my out-of-touchness with others, chances are, I would have become more and more out of touch with myself; I would have become confused, fearful, inadequate—only a remnant of my former self and perhaps even, who knows, a seedy, demented old man.

I realized in that time alone, as never before, how essential love is to the human condition. Without it we can exist, perhaps, but certainly not *live*. Without love, life is an empty, pointless, and, in many cases, even impossible affair.

I once watched a man murder
a beautiful and intelligent woman.
It wasn't, mind you, a crime of
passion in which he took her life

with a knife or gun in a single
explosive moment of blinding
rage. It was, rather, a crime
absolutely devoid of passion,

a murder within the law and over
a long period of time, four and
a half decades. It was murder
by indifference and neglect.

. . .

Once when Thomas Carlyle was holding forth at great length before a distinguished visitor, with his wife Jane Welsh listening attentively, he paused in his pontifical monologue. Turning to his devoted and long-suffering wife he said, "Jane, don't breathe so loud." Not long afterward Jane stopped breathing altogether. When Carlyle read her private journal, he discovered that his failure in kindness hurt her mortally. She died of emotional starvation; she craved and was denied love and considerateness. "If I had only known," moaned the miserable philosopher. But he should have known![4]

—David A. MacLennan

I was talking with a middle-aged clerical worker in a large hospital. "I've received two compliments today," she beamed, "and I'm walking on air!"

I know the feeling. Only the other day I received a note of appreciation from my superior. Completely unexpected, it was a warm and generous tribute. I filed it away as a pick-me-up to which I can turn in some despondent time.

I am reminded of the little boy who said to his father, "Let's play darts. I'll throw and you say, 'Wonderful!'"

I have never been quite so open about it, but I need that, too: "Wonderful!" Possibly as much as I need anything, I need to be valued, to know that my life counts for something in the eyes of others.

Without that, the appreciation of others and self and life itself (in that order), what point in living?

> I can live for two months on a good compliment.[5]
>
> —Mark Twain

A Vermont farmer, so the story goes, was sitting one evening with his wife on the porch of their home. As they looked out over the green and gentle valley in which they had spent the whole of their married life, not a word was spoken. Finally, however, the farmer broke the long, companionable silence. "Sarah," he said, "we've been through a lot of ups and downs in our forty years together, and sometimes when I think of what you've meant to me, it's all I can do to keep from telling you."

Like that good but tongue-tied man, some of us have great difficulty in giving expression to the love that we so deeply feel and that people so deeply need. We suffer, said Kierkegaard, from shutupness.

> There are few, very few, people with whom I am really friends. I have crowds of acquaintances, many people whose company I enjoy, but there are very few with whom I am really intimate. I think that I would seem to be a friendly, open person, but there are very few people with whom I am on first name terms, and I am a little shocked at the modern habit of indiscriminately greeting people with a kiss when they meet us.
>
> Because I was a parish minister for years, and have been a teacher for still more years, many people have at one time or another opened their hearts to me—and I do not think that I ever revealed anyone's secret to anyone else. People used to say to my wife: "He'll have told you such and such a thing," only to find that I had not mentioned it even to her. But I wonder if there is anyone to whom I would open my heart. Margot Asquith said that she could never talk to Balfour about religion. "He had," she said, "a little private property in his mind, in which was written at the portal, 'Trespassers forbidden.'"

I think that I am rather like that. There was an older minister for whom I had a very great respect and affection; he was a mystic and a saint and a very great soul. But he talked a great deal about his own faults and self-revilings, and he expected others to be as open. You would go and see him, and he would say: "I'm so glad to see you; I've been wanting a talk with you. Come and slap your soul on the table and let's open our hearts to each other." And it always made me slightly sick so that instead of talking I would clam up in silence. All this is perhaps mixed up with the fact that I dislike being touched, except by a very few people. In some ways I am a very gregarious person, what Dr. Johnson called a clubbable man, but somehow I like to keep my distance, and I like a decent reticence.[6]

—William Barclay

Last night a couple of incidents occurred within minutes of each other, two moments which, in their juxtaposition, provide a harsh contrast.

First, Enid hugged me. Scores of people were milling around and a small group of us were talking in a corner. Paul, Enid's husband, was one of the group. I mentioned how much I had appreciated a choral performance Paul had conducted a few evenings earlier. Joyously, and characteristically, Enid threw her arms around me and hugged me. It hadn't been a good day. I was tired and a little blue. But Enid helped change that. Her brief, affectionate gesture blessed the end of the day.

Then, moments later, Wallie came up to me and said, "Can we talk?"

"Sure."

"Alone?"

"Let's step outside."

Wallie, it developed, had just undergone a shattering experience. He needed help. Words, I knew were inadequate. I longed to embrace and comfort him. But I didn't, partly because there were so many people around. I did, however, manage, somewhat awkwardly, to put my hand on his shoulder. He clung to it as though it were his only hope.

Still, I failed Wallie. In my stupid Anglo-Saxon reserve, I denied him the love that reaches out and gathers its object into its arms.

> For thousands of years religion has been aware of the tremendous power that resides in touch. The Founder of Christianity was constantly in touch with people, especially when He was trying to help or reassure them. When children ran to Him, the Bible tells us that He took them in His arms. When He wanted to heal a leper or restore a blind man's sight, He touched them. At the Last Supper, He washed His disciples' feet. Some people say that this was to teach them a lesson in humility, but I believe it was more than that. Words were not enough to show the depths of His love; there also had to be touch.[7]
>
> —Smiley Blanton

Psychologist Sidney M. Jourard once studied the behavior of couples in cafés in various parts of the world. In San Juan, Puerto Rico, he noted, men and women, obviously paired, touched each other an average of 180 times per hour. In Paris couples touched almost as often, 110 times per hour. In a city in Florida, however, in a café catering mostly to middle-class whites, couples touched only twice an hour. In London, Jourard observed, couples didn't touch at all.

But while it is true of our WASPish society in general, it is especially true of us men that, by and large, we are an undemonstrative lot. Having been taught almost from infancy that to be masculine means to be cool, controlled, and self-contained, many of us have real difficulty in expressing our deepest feelings, love included. Fear, misery, anger, inadequacy, grief—all these feelings, and others too, are diligently hidden behind a mask of iron inscrutability.

Across the Atlantic, Englishmen greet one another with a polite handshake. Only twenty-one miles away, on the other side of the Channel, Frenchmen salute their male friends by kissing them robustly on both cheeks. In our habitual reserve, we North American males are far more English than French. Not for us the *abrazo*, the bear hug our Latin counterparts use as a form of greeting. God forbid.

One of our inhibiting fears, certainly, is that others will read a sexual meaning into a purely platonic statement or gesture.

In our sex-obsessed society, people see sex everywhere—in the media, in the arts, even in broad daylight in public places. So they can scarcely be blamed for seeing sex where there is no sex—in a touch, a hug, a kiss that is completely devoid of any erotic significance.

Well aware of this suspicious attitude, we refrain from expressing the love that can be so easily misinterpreted. Better to be cautious, we think, than to be labeled "a sexpot" or "a dirty old man."

> We want to touch—and a culture that has placed "a tabu on tenderness" leaves us stroking our dogs and cats when we may not stroke each other. We want to be touched—and often we dare not say so, but must go to the hospital for massage or physiotherapy or a doctor's examination. We are starved for the laying on of hands.[8]
>
> —Grace Stuart

In a fearful and guarded society, the simple act of loving requires a certain type of courage. It is not the kind of courage that enables people to scale precipitous mountains or sail solo around the world. It is a quieter, essentially unselfish courage, and far more necessary than its more brawny counterpart. In a hungry world, starved for food on three continents and starved for love in every quarter, the courage to love, much more than mere derring-do, is urgently and desperately needed.

7

LET GO AND LET GOD

Some people, said William James, are much more likely candidates for conversion than others; some need it, others don't.

I agree. Some people, it seems, are so *together*, so essentially "in tune with the Infinite," that to make some massive alteration in their way of life would only be to spoil a good thing.

I think of Neil, who, in terms of temperament, is one of the most fortunate people I know. Right from day one, he has gone sailing through life with a bare minimum of fuss and frustration. True, he isn't perfect. Like everyone, he has his faults and failings. But they are so minor and so few that to suggest that he is in need of a major overhaul would be sheer nonsense.

On the other hand, there are the much less fortunate who do need conversion. Life for them, for whatever reasons, is a troublesome, difficult business that from time to time becomes downright impossible.

When I was in my late thirties, I was, in one sense, in excellent health. I exercised each morning, strenuously. I could hike for hours and swim for miles. But at the same time something was seriously wrong: I was unable to do my work.

Within a few minutes after I began work, there would be a tightness in my chest, a constriction that soon became such a relentless ache that a couple of hours later, absolutely exhausted, I would have to go back to bed. I spent my whole day, every day, going from bed to desk and from desk to bed, over and over again.

I went to see a physician friend. "I have no energy, no stamina," I said. "I'm working less than half time, but even so I'm wrung right out."

He put me through an exhaustive battery of tests, then shared his findings: There was nothing organically wrong. The trouble must be elsewhere. Attitudinal, perhaps?

I went on with my work, but nothing changed. I tried everything I knew, everything from yoga to self-analysis to affirmative prayer, but I went from bad to worse. I was a broken, defeated wreck.

Finally one night, in my study upstairs, I fell to my knees, driven there because there was nowhere else to go, and in the darkness began pouring out my heart in silent prayer. At first, unspoken though it was, it was a long, agonizing wail of helplessness and need. From there it drifted somehow into a confession of sin, but one far different from any I had ever offered before. My acknowledgment of some of the more obvious sins, it seemed, triggered the recognition of others, a few at first and then more and still more—sins of the spirit, most of them, profoundly subtle and overwhelming in their sheer multitude. As C. S. Lewis put it, "I found what appalled me; a zoo of lusts, a bedlam of ambitions, a nursery of fears, a harem of fondled hatreds. My name was legion."[1]

The catharsis went on and on for, I suppose, close to an hour and left me utterly drained. More, it was a process that brought me face to face for the first time with all the sludge and poison in the human soul.

At last—still, apparently, following some kind of leading—I concluded the prayer by offering up my shabby, exhausted self. "I can no longer manage my life," I said. "I've tried, but it hasn't worked. I've been battered at every turn, and now I have no other option. I'm giving my life over to You. Do with it whatever You will."

There was no thunderclap, no blinding light. There was, however, a priceless gift: a strange, ineffable peace that came over me, a healing that within minutes filled my whole being. I went to bed, slept like a child, and wakened the next morning a new person.

A unique experience? For me, yes, but not in the annals of faith. Recorded there are the experiences of a vast number of people, men and women of every time and place, who, in their confusion and pain, abandoned self-determination and in so doing were amazingly blessed.

The one principle of hell is—"I am my own."[2]

—George MacDonald

In hell itself hell can your heaven be,

If there, says God, you give your will to me.[3]

—Angelus Silesius

In his will is our peace.[4]

—Dante Alighieri

I don't know Who—or what—put the question, I don't know when it was put. I don't even remember answering. But at some moment I did answer *Yes* to Someone—or Something—and from that hour I was certain that existence is meaningful and that, therefore, my life, in self-surrender, had a goal.[5]

—Dag Hammarskjöld

One of Sir Wilfred Grenfell's scrapbooks included a verse by Jonathan Swift:

We are God's favored few,
All others will be damned,
There is no place in heaven for you,
We can't have heaven crammed.

From time to time I meet people with that attitude. I met one not long ago, a man who reminded me of one of Mark Twain's sketches: "A solemn, unsmiling, sanctimonious old iceberg that looked like he was waiting for a vacancy on the Trinity."[6]

Christians, he declared, are the only ones who qualify for admission into the kingdom of heaven. Muslims and Hindus, Buddhists and Jews? No way.

I disagreed.

He shot right back, predictably, with the oft-quoted verse that, in speaking of Jesus, says, "There is salvation in no one else, for there is no other name under heaven given among men by which we must be saved."[7]

I didn't argue—it would have been futile. But I wish there were a way of convincing such people that Christians don't have a monopoly on grace. I wish they could see that Love is not narrow, selective, exclusive; Love is universal; Love reaches down to, and delivers, people of all faiths—and of none at all.

Conversion—being a matter of discovering the reality of God—occurs in all times and places, in all religions and outside of religion as well.[8]

—Emilie Griffin

Converted though I was, I remain much the same person I have always been: willful, stubborn, perverse; tainted by selfishness and pride; a thousand miles and more from the kingdom of the pure in heart.

In theological terms, I have been justified, yes, but not sanctified. Not by a long shot.

However, even though my life has not changed much on the surface, it has changed significantly at a deeper level. For I *know* now. I know that there is a Power, a Benevolence capable of redeeming even the most broken life, a Power awaiting an invitation that ultimately, whether in time or eternity, we are bound to extend. In that knowledge, I find, there is towering hope, and in that hope, it seems to me, we turn the corner; we begin to change and advance, to develop and grow.

> The fact is that if a convert has certain neurotic dispositions—towards fearfulness and worry, towards anger, towards moodiness and depression—these psychological dispositions remain after conversion and must be dealt with as they were before. It is true that believing in God makes a difference; it makes it possible to begin the conquest of these negative feelings with a new confidence. But the conversion—which is a passage from unfaith to faith—does not automatically convert the emotions as well. What it does is provide a hope which the convert previously lacked: first, that the universe makes sense, and second, that it is possible to rely on God for help, when on his own he has been powerless to rule his destiny or his feelings. But the act of conversion is not the same as the fact of getting better. . . .
>
> What has changed is not ourselves but our view of ourselves and where we stand with relation to the rest of the universe. To the extent that the universe now seems to us animated with God's energy and life, shot through with his tender affection and love, we may be able to make a beginning in the conquest of despair, anger, irritability, unkind words and thoughts towards others, promiscuity, dishonesty, and other destructive habits of thought and behavior with which we have been struggling unsuccessfully up to now. But conversion is no

guarantee of emotional well-being. Some of the holiest people who walked this earth were troubled with psychological trials and illnesses.[9]

—Emilie Griffin

In many a life the self is so largely identifed with some particular thing that the self cannot be relinquished without also relinquishing that thing, whatever it is.

I may, for instance, be a golf addict, out on the fairways every evening and every weekend. Golf is my raison d'être, my passion, my joy. But, in its obsessiveness, golf is also a curse. It is eating into my work, souring my marriage and, in general, ruining my life.

The solution? There is only one solution: Give up my life. But then I cannot really give up my life without giving up golf, for basically golf *is* my life.

For someone else, of course, the problem may be quite different. For Bill it may be a job in defense research, for Eva an illicit relationship, for Harry an ambition that has dominated his life for decades and that, in its unrealizability, has almost destroyed him.

In every bedeviled life, though, the thing that must be relinquished spells security, pleasure, hope; it represents some great need. Excising the thing, therefore, that is so central to our existence is painful in the extreme. It is like going through an amputation or divorce. It hurts like hell.

It remains true, however, that in many, many situations, heaven can be reached only by way of hell.

"There is always something they insist on keeping, even at the price of misery. There is always something they prefer to joy—that is, to reality."[10]

—C. S. Lewis

We bring our lives into line with the will of God and are overwhelmed by a sense of joy and peace. Life is beautiful, all sunshine under a cloudless sky.

Unfortunately, however, it doesn't last. Bit by bit, we slip, we fall away, we revert—to some extent at least—to what we were prior to our conversion.

It is easily explained: Almost inevitably, our spiritual recovery leads to the self-sufficiency or pride that eventually gets us in trouble.

Once back on our feet, we say to ourselves, "I'm fine now. I can manage quite nicely on my own." We reclaim the self so recently relinquished. But what happens then, of course, is that once again our mismanaged lives go into decline.

No, say the saints, true conversion is not just a once-and-for-all experience, however dramatic an upheaval it may be. As a matter of fact, that is only the beginning. Conversion, they say, if it is to amount to anything, must be followed by, must be reinforced and furthered by, thousands upon thousands of miniconversions. Conversion is ongoing; it is not only an event, it is also a process.

C. S. Lewis made the point when he said:

> The proper good of a creature is to surrender itself to its Creator—to enact intellectually, volitionally, and emotionally, that relationship which is given in the mere fact of its being a creature. . . . In the world as we now know it, the problem is how to recover this self-surrender. We are not merely imperfect creatures who must be improved: we are, as Newman said, rebels who must lay down our arms. . . . To surrender a self-will inflamed and swollen with years of usurpation is a kind of death. . . . Hence the necessity to die daily: however often we think we have broken the rebellious self we shall still find it alive.[11]

I have a friend who, as Lewis would put it, dies daily. Once, years ago, he was resoundingly converted. But it didn't stop there. He gets up now an hour before the rest of the family, as he has been doing for years, and goes into the kitchen for his "quiet time." He sits down at the table, pencil and paper before him, and in the quiet of the early morning listens for the "still small voice," the nudgings of the Spirit. When such a prompting comes, he makes a note of it. It may be something as mundane as "Write Aunt Ethel" or as momentous as "Resign." Then during the day he acts on those various biddings.

His life now, after all those years of obedience, is a beautiful, beautiful statement.

> I have chosen to call the experience of conversion a turning, not only because that word so simply renders into English the sense of the Latin *conversio* and the Greek *metanoia*, but also because it has not one but both

of the meanings for conversion which I intend. There is "first conversion"—that upheaval in our minds and hearts which we resolve when we first acknowledge the Lord and give ourselves to him. That is turning in the sense of a turnabout: a reversal, a change of course. Beyond that first conversion—as many converts learn to their surprise—there is another turning which is to last our whole life long. That is turning in another sense: transformation. In *Mere Christianity* Lewis says:

> Every time you make a choice you are turning the central part of you, the part that chooses, into something a little different from what it was before. And taking your life as a whole, with all your innumerable choices, all your life long you are slowly turning this central thing into a creature that is in harmony with God, and with other creatures, and with itself, or else into one that is in a state of war. . . . Each of us at each moment is progressing to the one state or the other.[12]

—Emilie Griffin

8

INSUFFICIENCY—AN INVITATION TO LOVE

From the helpless dependence of infancy to the determined independence of adolescence, from there to the interdependence, the give-and-take of maturity, and finally perhaps, completing the cycle, to the enforced dependence of advanced age—it is the old, old road, beaten hard by the footsteps of countless generations, the route we travel on our way from cradle to grave.

But what sometimes happens, unfortunately, is that we bog down in a particular stage of human development, or skip it entirely . . .

The excessively dependent person. She is an only child, born of wealthy parents who were crowding forty and desperate for an heir. She herself is an adult now, but one thing hasn't changed: Her parents still assume responsibility for every aspect of her life, still see to it that everything is done for her, everything provided. For over twenty years now, she has never had to struggle with difficult decisions, never had to struggle and stretch. She has been pampered and indulged to the *n*th degree. In all that smothering love, however, there has been an implicit message: "We're doing all this for you because we doubt your capability; we don't trust you." Predictably, she has never learned to trust herself. Bright though she is, and beautiful, her self-confidence is minimal. She is, and probably will be for the rest of her life, a leaner, a dependent, a clinging vine.

The excessively independent person. He had an absentee father, a man who was away from home for weeks at a stretch. His mother was an exceptionally capable person, but cold. In all probability, she had never wanted her son. He no doubt sensed her attitude, even as a small child, and began saying to himself (if not at a conscious level), "I don't need her any more than she needs me. I can manage quite nicely on my own." Which he proceeded to do. Beginning in his early teens, he worked after school and in the summertime to provide himself with pocket money, school supplies, and clothing. He put himself through university and became in time a successful professional, a self-made man. He remains, however, basically a loner, a proud, sensitive and fiercely independent person.

Carried too far,
thrift becomes meanness,
tolerance, moral indifference and honesty
an exercise in cruelty.

Carried too far,
industry is self-destructive,
generosity spoils its object
and tact obscures the truth.

Carried too far,
every virtue,
including independence and even moderation,
becomes a vice.

Seeing an elderly lady off at the station, I offer to help with her suitcase.

"No, thanks," she says brusquely. "I can carry it myself."

Granted, there is something commendable about her self-sufficiency, but, carried to those lengths, it certainly is not an attractive quality.

No, the more endearing person by far is the one who recognizes, perhaps intuitively, that we all need to be needed and who, accordingly, is quick to invite a helping hand.

Could it be, I wonder, that today's liberated woman is going a little too far when she brusquely rejects a man's courteous offer to be of assistance?

A young man recounts some recent experiences . . .

When he started out to pick up some papers that had been dropped by a secretary, she shouted, "I can do that! Don't make me out to be so helpless."

When he held a door open for a woman, she gave him an icy stare and said, "Do I look too weak to open a door for myself?"

When he offered his seat on a bus to a young woman who looked pregnant, her curt response was, "I'd rather stand."

Could it be that woman's newfound independence is sometimes carried to extremes? That a little chivalry is still in order?

Children are the first to admit their inadequacy and are, in their openness, the most endearing.

Said Joanie (whom I had met only a few minutes earlier) when we came to cross the street, "Please, hold my hand." Gladly!

Said Megan, "Grampie, will you please do up my beddons [buttons]?" Delighted!

Adult: "How old are you?"
Child: "Two."
Adult: "Oh, come now, you're older than that, aren't you?"
Child: "Yes . . . but I can't say fwee."

He asked for food and drink, for hospitality, for support in the cause. He asked for the use of a boat, a donkey, a room for a last meal with his friends.

He was of all men the most gifted, the most blessed, but at the same time there was about him a certain helplessness that utterly shames my posturing and pride.

I once served a certain church and did it well. I was vigorous and efficient. I cared for the people, yes, but at the same time I ran a tight ship.

After seven years I was followed by a man, a good friend actually, with an entirely different style. Loose. Easy. Reciprocal.

On the one hand, my friend ministers to people and on the other, he allows people to minister to him. In fact, he invites ministry. He shares his pain, his confusion, his need. The result? He receives help and support, gladly given, from every quarter.

People, I think, respected me—I know they blessed me with a lot of appreciation and affection. But those same people positively dote on my friend. He is a much loved man.

I think if I had it to do all over again, I would take a leaf out of my friend's notebook. I would be a little less self-sufficient, a little more human.

Mail-order brides are supposed to belong to another era, right? Pioneers, the old west, the days of yore?

Certainly it's not a concept that belongs in the 1980s, where life in the fast lane can leave you behind before you know it.

Well, meet Ray J. Brown, Jr., a 29-year-old shopkeeper here in rural Prince Edward Island. He'll give you a different story.

Brown placed an advertisement in recent editions of P.E.I.'s two daily papers explaining that he was looking for a wife.

This was no cryptic, teasing quickie in the personals column, mind you. The ad, running fully 2,500 words in fine print and costing $368, took up almost half of Page 2 and carried the heading "an important announcement to all husband hunters." Simply put, it was hard to miss.

In it, Brown catalogued the assets he felt important in a prospective mate, ran down the reasons he was looking for one this way and told as much about himself as an ad that size would allow (a lot).

He asked those women interested in meeting him to write him at the address he enclosed so he could see how he felt about their response and possibly set up a meeting.

It didn't take long to judge the response.

"I was afraid it would turn out that I'd get too many letters the way they came in at first and the phone calls I got," the Island-born bachelor told Southam News.

Predictably, many of the early responses were hoaxes, but within a matter of days the serious replies began to filter through.

One girl called him from Montreal (a sister had told her about the ad). Another girl with relatives on the Island called from Toronto; "I guess they're trying to get her married off," said Brown.

But it was on the Island, specifically Charlottetown, that the modern-day wife-hunter hit the real, uh, mother lode.

"I've met three women here now who would make wonderful wives," Brown said. "It's just a matter of choosing one of them."

He added that many other responses have come from people other than prospective husband-hunters.

"A lot of people have called just to say they think it's a good idea, that they're all in favor of what I'm doing.

"I wondered before whether I should be going about it this way but after this kind of response I'd do it again now," he said.

Brown's ad describes him as a devout Catholic who spent four years in an Ottawa seminary preparing to become a priest. He decided that a life of celibacy was not for him and moved back to the Island, although not without his religious convictions.

"I don't mind saying that I did a lot of praying about this," he said. "And it has strengthened my faith even more the way it's turned out."

The philosophical outlook that flows from his lengthy ad is a generous mixture of the Bible, Dear Abby, and Aesop's fables (the one about the fox who stopped trying to reach the grapes just beyond his grasp).

And, if nothing else, it's straightforward. As Brown says: "I'm a much better writer than talker."

The important thing to Brown is that he feels he has been able to meet girls who are precisely the type of people he sought.

And if the method he chose is the only way of making that come about, then what he's done has been successful.

As for the immediate future, he has taken a shine to one of the three Charlottetown girls in particular.

"I'll keep seeing her as much as I can," he said.

"I think I've found a wife."[1]

—Brian Butters

I have a friend who has been hit by one blow after another. Her marriage ended in divorce. She contracted lupus. Her heart failed, and a pacemaker was implanted. Even worse, she lost all but a small fraction of her sight—the result of medication mistakenly prescribed for her heart condition.

She has been at the brink of death a number of times. Her hold on life remains tenuous. But her spirit is amazing. Cheerful. Confident. With never the slightest trace of bitterness or self-pity. (I once heard her remark, almost as an aside, "I came to see that my blindness is really a gift.")

She is Director of Nursing at a hospital for the chronically ill and, in spite of her handicaps, a superb administrator. Steady. Efficient. Occasionally tough and always kind.

She is also a person who doesn't hesitate to say, "Will you please read this for me?" Or to reach out for someone's arm, someone who, in her darkness, can lead the way.

I know no one who so beautifully walks the *via media*, the middle way between excessive dependence on the one hand and excessive independence on the other. I know no one who better combines the self-sufficiency of an adult and the insufficiency of a child.

She is a superlative person, my friend.

9

THE IMPORTANCE OF BEING LAZY

In Harper's early days, a sturdy white horse harnessed to a vertical shaft furnished power to operate the presses. From seven in the morning until noon and from one o'clock to six the horse trudged around the shaft.

The time finally came when the Harper press horse, having earned an honorable retirement, was removed from his monotonous round and shipped away to enjoy a peaceful old age on Mr. Harper's farm. For the first few days the horse frisked about, delighting in his new-found leisure, but like many retired workers he soon began to miss his former occupation. His spirits were low, his appetite flagged.

One morning, so the story goes, when the seven o'clock whistle sounded on a nearby factory, the old horse trotted purposefully out to a large tree in the middle of the pasture and walked round and round it till the noon whistle blew. After an hour's siesta he again circled the tree till six and then sought his shed in the manner of one who has done a good day's work.

Every day thereafter as long as he was able to hobble he dutifully followed the same routine and gazed with scorn at the other horses frolicking about the pasture. Such capers were not for him; he had a job to do.[1]

—Harper's Magazine

Born and raised in a small town on the east coast, he
was a stocky, powerful man with a smile that could
illumine a whole room.
Energy? Zest? He had enough for a hundred people.
He was never tired, never discouraged and depressed.
He was *up*, all the time.

A man of enormous warmth, he had hundreds upon hundreds of friends.
People found him irresistible.
His wife was a godsend, a cultured, beautiful girl whom he adored as long as he lived.
She accompanied him to India, where, as a missionary, he became a legend.
An Air Force chaplain in World War II, he served on three fronts, flew as an observer on bombing missions ("It was a way of getting into the thick of it"), and was decorated by George VI in Buckingham Palace.
He came home, became an executive in church headquarters, and went on to serve some of the largest congregations in the land, speaking each Sunday to thousands of people.
He had no hobbies, really, no appreciation of literature, music, art.
He never took up photography, tennis, or golf.
His work was his whole life.
He gloried in it, reveled in it, poured into it every ounce of his energy and time.
He retired abruptly at the age of sixty-four because of his wife's precarious health and, without his work, was absolutely lost.
He missed the crowds, the spotlight, all the people in need of help.
He gardened, he puttered, he traveled.
He played Scrabble with his wife and friends.
But there were moments, many moments, when it all seemed empty, meaningless, futile.
He tried half-heartedly from time to time to get back into the professional mainstream, but it seemed that no one wanted an older man.
He felt useless, dated, rejected.
He endured nine years of retirement and then, in a single, shattering moment lost his beloved Ev.
Three months to the day after his wife's death, a broken, sorrowful man, he died himself, killed in a head-on collision.

His remains lie buried beside those of his wife on a beautiful site on the Pacific coast.
He was a dear, dear man.
He was my father.

I had seen workaholism before. I had seen it in my family and friends—yes, and also in myself. Still, I had no real understanding of the compulsion. I needed some answers.

One day, therefore, I did some research. I learned that one should not generalize; workaholics come in all shapes and sizes, all kinds and degrees. However, say the authorities, there are certain characteristics, certain distinguishing features, that workaholics tend to have in common. By and large, they say, but certainly not in every case . . .

- A workaholic is someone for whom inactivity is intolerable. Away from the job, he is restless and uncomfortable. Weekends are a continuing problem, often solved by going off into the den and burying himself in a pile of paperwork, brought home in his briefcase. Business trips are as infrequent as possible, and as brief—he dislikes being away from the office. Vacations? Either they are avoided or, if begun, aborted. Always, it seems, there is a phone call from the office, interpreted to mean that the company is about to fall apart, and then a hasty departure for home.
- A workaholic is someone without zest and enthusiasm, fire and passion. (But isn't his work a passion? No, not really. It is more a compulsion and, as such, devoid of music and laughter. A workaholic is someone who neither soars nor sings.)
- A workaholic is someone with a penchant for "polyphasic activity." Which is to say, he is often seen doing two or three things at once: watching TV, helping his children with their homework, and cutting his toenails, all at the same time.
- A workaholic is not a highly creative person. Chances are, in fact, he is a bit of a drone, someone whose thinking is flat and uninspired. (It might be otherwise, of course, if he took more time out for charging his batteries.)
- A workaholic is someone who, off the job, finds himself in a double bind: Either, he feels, the company will fall flat on its face in his absence or, God forbid, they will discover that they are doing just fine without him. He can't win.

- A workaholic is a doubtful, insecure person, unsure of others (he doesn't delegate responsibility) and unsure even of himself. At a deep level he is afraid that the fates are conspiring to engineer his collapse.
- A workaholic is someone with little or no appreciation of the present. He is a future-oriented person, whose whole life is slanted toward tomorrow, whenever that happens to be—the blissful day when all his dreams will be realized. (Only, of course, that day never comes.)
- A workaholic is someone who may give the impression of confidence and strength but who, beneath it all, is deficient in self-esteem.
- A workaholic is someone whose relentless activity is founded in part on a deep, unconscious reluctance to come face to face with himself. (Aldous Huxley said of such people, "They intoxicate themselves with work so they won't see how they really are.")
- A workaholic is someone who has great difficulty in letting go (of other things as well as his work) and leaving everything in the lap of the gods. He is a person long on conscientiousness but low in trust.

In a hard-driving and highly competitive society, we have been taught to equate hard work with success and success with fulfillment. In a host of instances, however, the success spells only emptiness and disillusionment.

A person toils away for years on end and then, confronted in the depths of his or her own heart with the question "Was it worth it?", whispers "No."

A man said it eloquently in the third century B.C.: "Then I considered all that my hands had done and the toil I had spent in doing it, and behold, all was vanity and a striving after wind, and there was nothing to be gained under the sun."[2]

> I bought the idea that if I could make a lot of money, live in a big home, be in charge of hundreds of employees, I'd be a success. I told myself that I'd pay whatever price it took to get to that point because once there I'd be happy and life would be satisfying.
>
> So I drove myself. My workday started at 5:30 A.M. and ended about 9 P.M. I was in the investment business. I founded a mutual fund and made a lot of money. I had a

home in San Francisco and a company apartment in New York. But I was more unhappy than when I started out. My marriage went on the rocks. My relationships with my children were strained.

> I looked around and saw a great many other top executives for whom life wasn't satisfactory either. They were taking extraordinary risks with their lives just to make a living. I thought, "God, that really doesn't make sense."
>
> Finally, I let go of a lot of values that I'd erroneously thought were correct. I'm 44 now, and I know if I hadn't become aware of what was happening to me, I wouldn't live to see 50.[3]
>
> —Christopher J. Hegarty

We had dealings from time to time, but I never came to know him. He was a distant man, unapproachable and all wrapped up in his work.

At home there were serious difficulties. His wife was in therapy, and his children, too, were having problems.

Eventually the marriage collapsed. It was predictable, in fact almost inevitable, and extremely painful.

Afterward I talked with his wife. She was hollow-eyed and thin, still shaky and tense. My heart went out to her.

"How did it happen?" I asked. "What went wrong?"

"Well, basically," she said, "he was just never around. All he did was work."

Like the more publicized addictions, workaholism can be the cause of a lot of pain. People devastated. Families shattered. Homes destroyed.

According to Carl Jung, a person has only a certain amount to invest in the whole business of life; one has only so much of energy and time, so much of intensity and love.

Some people, Jung went on to say, pour everything into a particular area of life—into their work, for instance—with the result that they have nothing left to invest in, say, music and art, in family relationships, in the life of the spirit. Far from being evenly developed, well rounded human beings, said Jung, these people end up imbalanced and lopsided, in some cases grotesquely so. Bent out of shape. Deformed.

Others, however, spread themselves much more evenly across the board. Work claims part of their time, and family a part. Hobbies and games, holidays and books, humanitarianism and faith—these, too, claim their attention, with impressive results. Look to these people, said Jung, if not for glittering professional accomplishment, for *personal* success. Look to them for examples of what it means to be truly and fully human.

> Thus the heavens and the earth were finished, and all the host of them. And on the seventh day God finished his work which he had done, and he rested on the seventh day from all his work which he had done.[4]

Mamie Eisenhower once reported to Dr. William Judd, her husband's physician, that when the President went to bed tired and worried, his prayer went something like this: "Lord, I've done the best I can today, and I'm grateful for your help. Doubtless I've muffed a few. You take over from here." Having done that, said Mrs. Eisenhower, "He just turns over and goes to sleep."

Eisenhower had a rare gift for relinquishing the cares of his office. In fact, it was this very attitude that his critics equated with irresponsibility. People complained that he didn't take the presidency seriously enough; he spent too much of his time out on the golf course.

More recently, however, a number of political commentators and historians have changed their minds. Walter Cronkite, for one, said that he first knew Eisenhower during the war and saw him often in subsequent years. Never, though, did he think much of him "either as a general or a President" until the post-White House years when he came to the conclusion that Eisenhower was actually "a brilliant man." Other authorities, too, are now saying that Eisenhower was one of the better presidents of the twentieth century.

Nixon, on the other hand, was an intensely political man, totally immersed in the presidential role. He had no hobbies to speak of. His work was everything. Nothing else mattered. But, needless to say, it was a disastrous presidency.

A friend pointed to a similar contrast in pre-War days. Hoover, he observed, was one of the most diligent presidents ever but, whether rightly or wrongly, was labeled one of the architects of the Depression. Roosevelt, next in the line of succession, was a far more blithe and carefree individual who, perhaps in part for that very reason, enjoyed a much more successful presidency.

It seems that a distinct advantage in the presidency is the ability to strike a balance between involvement and detachment, a balance between doing too much and doing too little.

His ministry lasted
a mere three years,
perhaps even less,
before it ended,
predictably,
in agony
and disgrace.
But, amazingly,
he was able to
laugh and rest
and play;
he made time
for banquets, weddings
and parties,
time for
going off by himself
into the solitude
for days on end,
there to find
his spirit replenished,
his body renewed.

I see now that those who sit lightly on their work are essentially humble persons. They don't suffer from self-importance, don't take themselves too seriously. They don't see themselves as indispensable—the center of a particular universe, the pivot on which everything stands or falls.

I see, too, that those who can easily disengage themselves from their labors are also trusting persons. They *believe.* They believe in others, in their ability to carry the load, and, perhaps more important, they believe (whether they know it or not) in the Other. They believe in life, in the process, in the future, in the ultimate okayness of things.

I think of Martin Luther, who used to say, "While I drink my little glass of Wittenberg beer, the gospel runs its course." Luther recognized the importance of his role, but at the same time he didn't see himself as indispensable. Luther recognized that, after all, he was only a small cog in the eternal process, recognized that while he was eating and drinking and sleeping and playing, the universe, in good hands, was unfolding as it should.

It has happened time and again, especially in my writing . . .

I push myself morning, noon, and night for days on end, with the result that I end up tense, in fact all tied up in knots, and exhausted. I have nothing left, neither an ounce of energy nor a single creative idea. I am as empty and dry as Sahara. Then? Of necessity, I give up. I lose myself in rest or play. Hours pass, sometimes even days, and then it happens: Out of nowhere I am hit by some startling idea, perhaps even a whole chain of ideas, that somehow opens the floodgates and starts everything flowing again.

It has happened so many times that I no longer push myself beyond a certain point. I know now when I reach that point, and when I reach it, I stop. I wait. I trust. And the trust is always justified. Sooner or later, illumination comes and, with it, release. I am off and running, and grateful and happy.

It happens sometimes in the early hours of the morning. As I sleep, an idea, a scheme, an outline begins developing in the depths of my unconscious mind. Gradually it floats up into my awareness and I waken. I get out of bed, go off to my study, write it down, then go back to sleep. (Later, in all probability, I will have to do some fine tuning—but surprisingly little.)

It happens at other times in my waking hours. I am walking along, perhaps, thinking of nothing in particular, when suddenly there comes the key, the answer to some problem with which I have been wrestling on and off for days.

Whenever it happens, whether day or night, I feel a sense of delightful surprise and, with it, a surge of gratitude that in its own way is a prayer.

> Now this intensity of awareness is not necessarily connected with conscious purpose or willing. It may occur in reverie or in dreams, or from so-called unconscious levels. An eminent New York professor related an illustrative story. He had been searching for a particular chemical formula for some time, but without success. One night,

while he was sleeping, he had a dream in which the formula was worked out and displayed before him. He woke up, and in the darkness he excitedly wrote it down on a piece of tissue, the only thing he could find. But the next morning he could not read his own scribbling. Every night thereafter, upon going to bed, he would concentrate his hopes on dreaming the dream again. Fortunately, after some nights he did, and he then wrote the formula down for good. It was the formula he had sought and for which he received the Nobel prize. . . .

But let it be said immediately that unconscious insights or answers to problems that come in reverie do not come hit or miss. They may indeed occur at times when we alternate play with work. But what is entirely clear is that they pertain to those areas in which the person consciously has worked laboriously and with dedication . . . that is, *the insight never comes hit or miss, but in accordance with a pattern of which one essential element is our own commitment.*[6]

—Rollo May

When Leonardo da Vinci was working in the little church of Santa Maria delle Grazie on his incomparable canvas of the Last Supper, so the story goes, he used to spend hours at a time in meditation, out in the cloister.

"He's just wasting time," the monks complained. "He's taking advantage of his contract."

So charged, the artist answered, "When I pause the longest, I make the most telling strokes with my brush."

Let me close this chapter by quoting at considerable length from *Take It Easy*, one of my previous books:

. . . it often happens that the less we try, the better we do.

If, for instance, I am out golfing with one of my friends, and if at the end of the first nine I am down five strokes, and if I step up to the tenth tee, resolved, "This time, by golly, I'm going to out-drive him by a good twenty-five yards and then go on from there to even the score in a great hurry," I am almost certain to flub my drive and fall even further behind.

In other sports, too, the same thing is true: The laurels often go to those who play much of the game in an amazingly relaxed way.

I am not suggesting, of course, that a topflight athlete—say a professional basketball player—does not try hard. He most certainly does. Chances are that, like the others in his league, he is a fierce competitor. But the point is that, even though he puts a great deal of himself into the game, he does not go flat-out every minute he is on the floor. He paces himself. He husbands his strength and speed for the really critical moments. Also, as he himself might put it, he does not "press." He seldom extends himself to the absolute limit. In fact, for much of the game he seems to be merely coasting. But, even though it may not be apparent to some, it is this very attitude, this relaxed approach, that constitutes one of the most significant factors in his superb performance.

For centuries the Far Eastern masters of Zen Buddhism have maintained that in every respect, not only mentally and spiritually but physically too, we operate most effectively when we are yielding, compliant, relaxed. Judo is a case in point. Deeply rooted in Zen philosophy, judo is not, as so many westerners believe, an exercise in super-aggressive brutality. On the contrary, students of judo are taught how, as a boxer might put it, to backpedal, to roll with the punches. They are taught how to give way, how to yield. They are taught a number of techniques through which they allow their opponents to be the aggressors and, in the final analysis, to defeat themselves by the onrush of their own aggression.

In the sphere of intellectual activity the same truth holds: again and again people succeed not by striving more but by striving less. They succeed by easing up, by slacking off.

At one time or another, for instance, all of us have made a concentrated effort to remember a particular name, but without the slightest success. We tried and tried, cudgeling our brains for minutes on end. But no matter how hard we tried, we could not remember. Finally we gave up the attempt and went on with our business, and then it happened: there was a burst of illumination, one of those surprising occurrences of the so-called Aha Phenomenon. All of a sudden and all on its own, without the least effort on our part, the elusive name popped up out of the murky depths of our unconscious mind and presented itself for our use. . . .

It is significant, too, that time and again in the course of history people have been doing nothing in particular, merely daydreaming, when all of a sudden there dawned on them truths of immense importance. Archimedes lounging in a tub full of hot water, Newton sprawled out under an apple tree, Watts idly watching a boiling teakettle—these men were not trying to find the answers but, rather, were simply woolgathering when suddenly out of the blue there came to them ideas that have made a world of difference in human life. . . .

When we turn to the domain of the arts, we find once again that, while effort can be productive up to a certain point, beyond that point it tends to be futile and even counterproductive.

A few years ago, I remember, I set out to do some painting. My first attempt was a watercolor. A simple scene, it was a picture of a lighthouse on a bleak, windswept point. I spent only two or three hours on the painting but, much to my surprise, it turned out quite well. Encouraged by that first small success, I set out to paint a second picture, an abstract in acrylics. "But this time," I told myself, "I'm going to do something much more ambitious. This one is going to be a minor masterpiece." With that in mind, I spent several hours in drafting the picture, bought myself a large canvas and went to work. My technique could not have been more meticulous. I fussed over every move, labored over every detail. But somehow I just could not actualize the picture I had in mind. No matter how hard I tried, my painting would not turn out as I wanted. Finally I consigned the attempt to the garbage can and, discouraged but not defeated, began again. This time, too, the same thing happened. The more I struggled over my creation, the more dissatisfied, frustrated, and generally unhappy I became. Once again my would-be masterpiece ended up with the rest of the family's rubbish. But as if that were not enough, I did the very same thing still another time—proof, I suppose, of my stubborn refusal to recognize that in art, as in so many other areas of life, effort too plentifully applied tends to be self-defeating. . . .

In the performing arts, too, people function most effectively when, instead of putting themselves under all kinds of pressure, they ease up and allow the music or the message to flow through them freely and from somewhere far beyond.

Recognizing this, a wise director will sometimes counsel actors to take a few deep breaths, let their muscles go limp and, in their whole approach, be vastly more relaxed.

On the night *The Diary of Anne Frank* was to open on Broadway, Garson Kanin, the director, went backstage to wish the cast good luck. Behind the scenes he found Joseph Schildkraut, one of the actors, in a highly agitated state. Schildkraut had performed well on the road, except perhaps for a slight tendency to overact. But prior to that first performance in New York City he was suffering from one of the worst attacks of the jitters he had ever experienced. Clutching his director's arm, he pleaded, "Say something to me that will help me. Say one thing. Please." In reply Kanin said just one quiet, reassuring word: "Less."[6]

10

LOVE LETS GO

"You fall in love," he said, "and you get kicked in the teeth. It happens every time."

He was exceedingly bitter but essentially right: to love is to be vulnerable; to love is to be eventually hurt.

A second-grade teacher in Milwaukee greeted her children at the beginning of a new term with an assignment to write a composition on "something important you learned during your vacation." Among the essays turned in was the following:

WHAT I LEARNED ON MY VACATION

DON'T GET PERCONEL WITH A CHICKEN

By Eloise Coleman

On my vacation I visited with my gran parents in Iowa and my gran father learned me don't get perconel with a chicken. My gran father has a few chickens and one was a chicken I got perconel with and gave the name Gene Autry. One day my gran mother deside to have stood chicken for dinner and says Orf you go out and kill a hen meening my gran father. I went with him and low and behold he took a poke with a wire on the end and reeched in the pen and got Gene Autry by the leg and pulled him out and before I could say a werd he rung his neck which pulls off his hed and he flops around on the grond back and forth without no hed on and I cryed. He was a brown one. Then he scalted him in hot water and picket the feathers of an saw me crying and says dont ever get perconel with a chicken. When we are at the dinner table he says it again so I ate some, a drumb stick. I dident say anything but it was like

> eating my own rellatives. So dont get perconel with a chicken, also a cow if you are going to eat it later. Also a caff.[1]
>
> —H. Allen Smith

". . . and so they were married and lived happily ever after."

I suppose I believed it as a child, but now, of course, I know better. I see that "ever after" is, at best, only a few decades. I see that sooner or later love must relinquish its object and be dissolved in grief.

I think of Janet and Paul, whom I visit each week. Paul is dying. Down through the years I have known a number of good men in ministry, very good men, but only a handful of saints. Paul is one of that handful, one of the most loved and admired men I know. Now, however, there is only a remnant of the old Paul, and that remnant is gradually ebbing away.

It pains Janet to see her husband's decline. In fact, it breaks her heart to see the body now inert, the mind now dulled, the spirit and warmth, once such a vivid flame, now only a small, occasional flicker.

I marvel at Janet's devotion. Every day, no matter how miserable the weather, she trudges over to the nursing home to be with her husband. She talks to him and helps feed him. She sits by his bed for hour after hour, even when he is asleep, as he is most of the time, or awake but largely unresponsive. "He knows I'm there," she says, "and I have the feeling it means a lot."

Janet is still resisting Paul's gradual disengagement from life, and that resistance, though less than it was, is emotionally punishing. Concerned friends keep saying, "Janet, you need to ease up. We're afraid you're going to collapse." What they are talking about is not so much the number of hours she spends at Paul's bedside as it is the nature of those hours, the intensity with which they are freighted, the hanging on.

Janet is letting go, as she knows she must, but she has never done a more difficult thing in her life.

> The reality is that all relationships inevitably will be dissolved and broken. The ultimate price exacted for commitment to other human beings rests in the inescapable fact that loss and pain will be experienced when they are gone, even to the point of jeopardizing one's physical

> health. It is a toll that no one can escape, and a price that everyone will be forced to pay repeatedly. Like the rise and fall of the ocean tides, disruptions of human relationships occur at regular intervals throughout life, and include the loss of parents, death of a mate, divorce, marital separation, death of family members, children leaving home, death of close friends, change of neighborhoods, and loss of acquaintance by retirement from work. Infancy, adolescence, middle age, old age—all seasons of life involve human loss.[2]
>
> —James J. Lynch

There is, of course, an alternative to love with its concomitant pain: no-love, the denial of love.

It sometimes happens, and understandably so: A person is hurt by love over and over again, with the result that love is finally renounced. "No, thanks," says the victim. "Not for me. Never again. It's too damned painful."

The fact is, though, that no-love, while it seems safe, is far more damaging than love. In time no-love renders a person an empty, dessicated shell, only a fraction of the onetime, not to mention potential, self.

Actually, we have no alternative; we must love. It is either love, along with pain, or gradual death.

> Love anything, and your heart will certainly be wrung and possibly be broken. If you want to make sure of keeping it intact, you must give your heart to no one, not even to an animal. Wrap it carefully round with hobbies and little luxuries; avoid all entanglements; lock it up safe in the casket or coffin of your selfishness. But in that casket—safe, dark, motionless, airless—it will change. It will not be broken; it will become unbreakable, impenetrable, irredeemable. The alternative to tragedy, or at least to the risk of tragedy, is damnation. The only place outside Heaven where you can be perfectly safe from all the dangers and perturbations of love is Hell.
>
> I believe that the most lawless and inordinate loves are less contrary to God's will than a self-invited and self-protected lovelessness.[3]
>
> —C. S. Lewis

Reluctant as we are to relinquish those we love to life, we are even more reluctant to relinquish them to death. Faced with the death of someone we love, we tend to cling like leeches.

I remember the hysterical widow who, during the committal service, had to be physically restrained from throwing herself into her husband's grave. I shall never forget her shrieking, demented behavior, her absolute refusal to say good-bye.

Usually, however, it happens at the hospital bedside. People urge those they love, those in the last stages of life, to make more of an effort to live: "Don't give up, honey! Hang in there. You'll see—we'll make it yet." Either that or they wring their hands and wail, "But you can't leave us! You just *can't*. What'll we ever do without you!"

God, give me grace, when the time comes, not to add to my beloved's pain by refusing my permission to die.

Brian P. was fifty, but looked younger. He was recovering from an operation in which part of his stomach was removed because of cancer. Afterward the man had been hopeful and looked forward to his retirement in a few years. Instead of improving, however, Mr. P. lost weight and grew increasingly weak. He became more and more depressed at the thought of his demise.

The man's wife continually assured him that nothing was wrong and that he would soon regain his former health and vigor. Still the man's condition worsened and soon forced him to enter the hospital again. This time malignant tumors were discovered in his lungs. Nevertheless his wife seemed to remain convinced he would recover, and during visits to the hospital she continually reminded him of his promise to buy a "retirement" home in the Southwest.

When the couple's daughter came home from college for a visit with her father she was visibly shocked to see his condition. "You have to get well," she told him. After the daughter departed, her father thought regretfully about her childhood and all the time he had spent away from his family involved in his business. He had limited his time at work after his first operation, but by that time his daughter had already gone away to school.

Although Mr. P.'s recovery was doubtful, and he was always in great pain, his family continually reminded him how much he was needed and how they expected a rapid improvement in his health. The nurses encouraged him to eat more, and his doctors kept talking to him about the possibility of another operation. Somewhat justifiably Mr. P. felt that there was nobody with whom he could talk about the seriousness of his condition.

One afternoon a hospital psychiatrist visited him and said that she would be available if he wanted to talk about anything. The patient spoke in a soft, weak voice and told her that each of his waking moments was agony because he had failed to fulfill his family's expectation. "I want to sleep, sleep, sleep and not wake up. How can a man die in peace when everyone wants him to get well?" he asked.

The psychiatrist then intervened with the family in an attempt to help them help the patient die more comfortably. She explained that the man was facing his impending death courageously, but their refusal to "let him go" was making it infinitely more difficult. The patient was ready to separate himself from this world, the psychiatrist said, so ordering additional medical treatment would only prevent him from finding the relief he sought in sleep.

Mr. P. apparently suffered much more from the feeling that he had disappointed his family than he did from the pain and physical discomfort of his disease. Once his relatives were able to accept the reality of the situation, they stopped trying to urge him back to health and the man was able to die in peace.[4]

—David Hendin

Part of a conversation from my recent past . . .

"It was the strangest thing," she said. "We fought his death, we fought it tooth and nail. But then it hit me. My God, I thought, we're just making him miserable!—we've got to let him go. So I said to him, 'It's OK, pet. Don't worry about us—we're OK now.' I was crying as I said it, but there's no doubt he got the message. I remember the way he—he kind of relaxed. It was as if he was free now, free to go. He smiled."

She went on: "He died that same afternoon and, you know, it was an easy death. Almost happy. I can't get over it."

> At first it might seem strange to insist that the dying need permission to do the inevitable. . . . But patients who feel any degree of human closeness or of responsibility to others, who had love in their lives and people near who needed them, require permission if death is to be peaceful. There is no other way to still feelings of guilt for going, for copping out on life, for becoming an emotional and financial burden and for that feeling of horrible helplessness inside.
>
> Reasonably sensitive persons know well and feel deeply the pain and sorrow their death will cause. They feel guiltily responsible when they know logically they are not. Each tearstained face, each wringing hand, each look of futility, pushes buttons of guilt inside a patient who cares. Always before there was a way out of guilt, an apology or explanation, a promise not to fail again, an act of special kindness in reparation. Because when dying there is only a single and unacceptable solution, permission becomes essential. . . .
>
> Clinical studies record a visible relief in patients when loved ones accept their dying without blame or despair. Other patients seem to survive beyond usual expectations, suffering ineffable pain, as if waiting like beggars for a "yes" from important people.[5]
>
> —Robert E. Kavanaugh

Psychologists speak of it as passive-dependence, this excessive clutching at people, this eternal hanging on.

I see it in Alice and Bernie (not their real names), who met not long ago (each, incidentally, on the rebound from a broken relationship) and who are now inseparable; holding hands, gazing into each other's eyes, so wrapped up in each other that they are almost totally oblivious to everyone else.

Alice and Bernie are lost without each other. After even the briefest of separations, they fling themselves into one another's arms, almost as if to say, "Thank God, we're safe now!" Apart from each other, they would say, they feel empty and unfulfilled; yes, and vaguely anxious and uneasy. But what they probably would not admit is that they also feel a little suspicious and threatened ("I wonder who's kissing her now"). At a deep level, Alice and Bernie are unsure of each other, just as they are unsure of themselves. At that same deep level, they are two anxious and insecure people, each of them partial and incomplete without the other.

Alice and Bernie say, "We love each other." But the truth is that they don't so much love as *need* each other.

> "When you require another individual for your survival, you are a parasite on that individual. There is no choice, no freedom involved in your relationship. It is a matter of necessity rather than love. Love is the free exercise of choice. Two people love each other only when they are quite capable of living without each other but *choose* to live with each other."[6]
>
> —W. Scott Peck

"Lovers," said C. S. Lewis,

> are normally face to face, absorbed in each other; Friends, side by side, absorbed in some common interest. . . . That is why those pathetic people who simply "want friends" can never make any. The very condition of having Friends is that we should want something else beside Friends. Where the truthful answer to the question *Do you see the same truth?* would be "I see nothing and I don't care about the truth; I only want a Friend," no Friendship can arise—though Affection of course may. There would be nothing for the Friendship to be *about*; and Friendship must be about something, even if it were only an enthusiasm for dominoes or white mice.[7]

Antoine de Saint-Exupéry echoed that sentiment when he wrote, "Love does not consist in gazing at each other but in looking outward together in the same direction. There is no comradeship except through union in the same high effort."[8]

Said Robert Runcie, Archbishop of Canterbury, speaking at the wedding of Prince Charles and Lady Diana, "Marriage is first of all a new creation for the partners themselves. . . . But any marriage which is turned in upon itself, in which the bride and groom simply gaze obsessively at one another, goes sour after a time. A marriage which really works is one which works for others."[9]

It follows, I think, that Friendship, as Lewis put it, or love will, when it becomes necessary, leave its partner and, sorrowful but self-sufficient, keep on trudging toward its chosen goal. After all, love's highest devotion is not to the love at its side but, in common with its partner, to the Love beyond.

> A good relationship has a pattern like a dance and is built on some of the same rules. The partners do not need to hold on tightly, because they move confidently in the same pattern, intricate but gay and swift and free, like a country dance of Mozart's. To touch heavily would be to arrest the pattern and freeze the movement, to check the endlessly changing beauty of its unfolding. There is no place here for the possessive clutch, the clinging arm, the heavy hand; only the barest touch in passing. Now arm in arm, now face to face, now back to back—it does not matter which. Because they know they are partners moving to the same rhythm, creating a pattern together, and being invisibly nourished by it.
>
> The joy of such a pattern is not the joy of creation or the joy of participation, it is also the joy of living in the moment. Lightness of touch and living in the moment are intertwined.[10]
>
> —Anne Morrow Lindbergh

If ever I saw nonpossessive love, it was in my mother; it was in the way—or, rather, in all the ways—she said to my father, "Go, Herb; go with my blessing."

Right from the beginning, they were in many ways a mismatched pair (which, I suppose, may partly account for the marriage—the mutual attraction of polar opposites).

She was slim and beautiful; quiet, cultured, refined. She loved books and music and art. Her home, wherever it happened to be, was always elegantly decorated and furnished. She was a lady, in the finest sense of the word, a lady of taste and quality and class.

Dad, on the other hand, was the proverbial rough diamond, a noisy, dynamic man of enormous gusto and zest. Born into a struggling family and raised in a small town, he never escaped his background. True, Mother's influence may have changed him a little, but not much. Even after forty years of marriage, he didn't have the foggiest idea who Rouault was, or dos Passos, or Martha Graham. Take him to the opera and he would squirm uncomfortably, to the symphony and he would fall sound asleep (something he could do at the drop of a hat). No, Dad's tastes were distinctly plebeian. His interests ran more to loud colors and Western movies, to bass fishing and gospel music.

To her immense credit, though, Mother never tried to change him, never tried to make him over. Other wives might struggle to smooth off the rough edges and give their husbands a little more polish and class, but not Mother. She let her husband be what he was. More than once, I saw her wince at Dad's gaffes; I saw her flush with embarrassment. But never once did I see her insisting that he change.

Too, she freed her husband to go wherever the spirit led.

Dad was a nomad, seldom home. Assignment after assignment kept him away from his family for weeks, months, and, in wartime, even years at a stretch. And Mother? Unfailingly, she let him go.

I remember a sad moment on the eve of my father's departure for overseas service in the early stages of the war. I wakened late that night and, through our open doorways, heard my parents in their room across the hall. Mother was sobbing inconsolably, Dad trying to comfort her. My mother was normally a staunch member of the stiff-upper-lip school. But that night, for the first time, I saw her other side; I saw how painful it was for her to keep saying good-bye. Yet say it she did, over and over again.

I remember also seeing them off at the airport about a year before Mother's death. Dad was recovering from a stroke—a broken, enfeebled man. In spite of it all, though, he had agreed to spend six months working in South Africa. Family and friends, his doctor included, had all tried to dissuade him, but to no avail. He was determined to go. As I watched this frail old man, my father, shuffling across an acre of terrazzo floor to see about some luggage, I turned to Mother and said, "Why didn't you put your foot down? Why didn't you just refuse to go?"

I shall never forget her reply: "No, I couldn't do that. I love him too much to tie him down."

Him that I love I wish to be
Free:

Free as the bare top twigs of tree,
Pushed up out of the fight
Of branches, struggling for the light,
Clear of the darkening pall,

Where shadows fall—
Open to the golden eye
Of sky:

Free as a gull
Alone upon a single shaft of air,
Invisible there,
Where
No man can touch,
No shout can reach,
Meet
No stare;

Free as a spear
Of grass,
Lost in the green
Anonymity
Of a thousand seen
Piercing, row on row,
The crust of earth,
With mirth,
Through to the blue,
Sharing the sun
Although,
Circled, each one,
In his cool sphere
Of dew.

Him that I love, I wish to be
Free—
Even from me.[11]

—Anne Morrow Lindbergh

11

GOOD-BYE TO GALLOPING AMBITION

What is it, the dominant impulse in human nature? Is it the urge for sex? Or the drive for authority and power, a drive born of the helplessness and inferiority of childhood? Freud maintained the former, Adler the latter.

I tend to agree with Adler (perhaps because I now view life through trifocals). More than anything, I think, we crave a certain status; we want to be able to chant, as we did in childhood, "I'm the king of the castle"; we want to be able to look down on all the others, much less privileged than ourselves.

> We all want to play Hamlet.[1]
>
> —Carl Sandburg

I often hear of the victims of, say, cancer, alcoholism, coronary thrombosis. But a group of whom I almost never hear, a whole army of people, is made up of all the casualties of excessive ambition.

I have talked with some of them lately, people who drive and punish themselves unmercifully—and even destroy themselves—in their relentless struggle to scale the giddy heights of Success.

If I am to be honest, though, I must admit that I see something of that same drive within myself. I doubt there is as much of it as there once was—I hope not. But it is still there, I know: a remnant, and sometimes more than a mere remnant, of the old, fierce desire to be somebody, to get ahead, to reach the top.

I see the same thing in our clan. I see so much of it, in fact, that I sometimes wonder if it is not a family curse. Where other families must cope with a legacy of hemophilia, senile dementia, or whatever, we Ashfords must deal, generation after generation, with this enormous, even pathological, appetite for power, possessions, prestige.

I wish we were free of it. I wish we could be content with a modest job, a modest home, a modest life. I wish we could be, in a word, *content*.

> There was once a lily that stood quite apart, near a little running brook, and was well acquainted with some nettles as well as a few other small flowers there in the neighborhood. The lily was, according to the Gospel's veracious description, more beautifully arrayed than Solomon in all his glory, beside being carefree and happy the whole day long. . . .
>
> But it happened one day that a little bird came and visited the lily; it came again the next day, and then it remained away for several days before it came again; which impressed the lily as being strange and inexplicable, inexplicable that the bird should not stay in the same place, like the small flowers—strange that the bird could be so capricious. But as so often happens, so too it happened to the lily, that because the bird was so capricious, the lily fell more and more in love with it.
>
> The little bird was a bad bird; instead of putting itself in the place of the lily, instead of rejoicing with it in its beauty and innocent happiness, the bird wished to make itself important by feeling its own freedom, and by making the lily feel its bondage. And not only this, the little bird was also talkative, and it would tell all kinds of stories, true and false, about how there were, in other places, very unusually magnificent lilies in great abundance; how there were joy and gaiety, fragrance, brilliant coloring, a song of birds, which far surpassed all description. . . .
>
> So the lily became troubled; the more it listened to the bird the more troubled it became. . . . Now it began to occupy itself with itself and with the circumstances of its life in its self-concern—so long was the day. . . . Said the lily, "My wish is not an unreasonable desire; I do not ask the impossible, to become what I am not, a bird, for

example; my desire is only to become a splendid lily, or even the most splendid one." . . .

At last it confided absolutely in the bird. One evening they agreed that the next morning a change should take place which would put an end to the concern. Early the next morning came the little bird; with its beak it cut the soil away from the lily's roots, so that it might thus become free. When this was accomplished, the bird took the lily under its wing and flew away. The intention was, of course, that the bird would take the lily to where the magnificent lilies bloomed; then the bird would again assist in getting it planted down there, to see if, through the change of soil and the new environment, the lily might not succeed in becoming a magnificent lily in company with the many, or possibly even an imperial lily, envied by all the others.

Alas, on the way the lily withered. If the discontented lily had been satisfied to be lily, then it would not have become concerned; if it had not become concerned, then it would have remained standing where it was—where it stood in all its beauty; had it remained standing, then it would have been precisely the lily about which the preacher spoke on Sunday, when he repeated the Gospel's words: "Consider the lily. . . . I say unto you that even Solomon in all his glory was not arrayed like it." . . .

And if a man, like the lily, is satisfied with the fact of being human, then he does not become ill from temporal concern; and if he does not become temporally concerned, then he continues to stand in the place appointed to him; and if he remains there, then it is truly so, that through being human he is more glorious than the glory of Solomon.[2]

—Søren Kierkegaard

Our raging appetite for superiority can, I learn, have its roots in unappreciative parents, in social rejection, in some real or imagined handicap, or, for that matter, in a combination of these and other factors—all of them fueled, of course, by our society's enormous devotion to "the bitch-goddess Success."

Ambition, I also discover, is a form of anger, born of profound personal insecurity, and, like all anger, an expression of hate.

Psychoanalyst Karen Horney spoke of compelling ambition as "a moving against people," a form of revenge. I hate people for what they have done to me, or failed to do for me. I am determined, therefore, that someday, by God, I'm going to show those bastards who's boss!

> Derogatory opinion is a fertile seed for ambition.[3]
>
> —Wayland F. Vaughan

"If the greedy person," said Benedict Spinoza, "thinks only of money and possessions, and the ambitious one only of fame, one does not think of them as being insane . . . but, factually, ambition and so forth are forms of insanity."

Insane or not, ambition is certainly a form of greed and, as such, the opposite of contentment.

Hugely ambitious people are, I think without exception, profoundly discontented people, forever grasping for more of this, that, or the other thing—the more that, they hope, will somehow fill the aching void at the heart of their lives.

It is odd how some criticisms *stick*, lodged in our minds because of their crisp and essential truth.

Years ago, I remember, Ian commented mildly that I was actually quite a greedy person. I was astounded. I hadn't been hotly pursuing fortune and fame. Upward mobility had never much mattered to me. What did he mean? But then I began to see: There was truth in the charge. I *was* greedy, only it was greediness of a different kind. What I coveted was meaning, fulfillment, satisfaction. Not for me the average, and often humdrum, life that so many people are compelled to lead. I wanted something different, something more spiritually rewarding. I wanted a rich *inner* life.

Ambition, it seems, wears many faces, some of them less crass than others but, at bottom, no less selfish.

> And James and John, the sons of Zebedee, came forward to him, and said to him, "Teacher, we want you to do for us whatever we ask of you." And he said to them, "What do you want me to do for you?" And they said to him, "Grant us to sit, one at your right hand and one at your left, in your glory."[4]

I know all too well that exorcising the demon of ambition is wickedly difficult. Once lodged in a person's heart, it can be evicted, or at least largely evicted, only by massive and continuing effort. True, time tends to whittle it down and weaken its grip; life has a way of disabusing us of our pride and destroying our illusions (which is to say, few people are as ambitious in their forties as they were twenty years earlier). But even so, dominating ambition remains one of the most powerful and tenacious evils with which many of us must cope.

As I reflect on galloping ambition, I come to the conclusion that two effective ways of dealing with the problem (apart, of course, from simple self-denial) are self-understanding and self-acceptance.

On self-understanding . . .

I listen to Mozart with the music pouring over me, drowning me in its sublimity, and I think Mozart was a child of destiny, someone *meant* to be a composer. Right from the day of his birth—even, for all I know, from the foundation of time—he was meant to be exactly what he was; he was meant to be *Mozart.*

I think too of people like Albert Einstein and Joan Sutherland, Luther Burbank and Mother Teresa, each of them so *right*, so monumentally effective in his or her field that, seeing them, we say to ourselves, Yes, that's where they belong; that's what they were meant to be.

I know a superb photographer for whom there is no distinction between work and play. His work—no, his art—is his joy, his passion, his life. He is another one of those people so marvelously in tune with the whole life-process that he seems to be fulfilling some transcendental intention.

It follows, I think, that for each of us there is a Plan, not perhaps a Plan of colossal proportions but a Plan nevertheless. A. is designed for medicine, B. for computer science, C. for motherhood, and so on.

Where so many of us go wrong, though, is that we don't correctly read the Plan for our lives. We read it, perhaps, in ignorance, including the ignorance of self; we read it through the eyes of others, people who mean well but whose perception of us is nowhere near the truth; we read it through a film of pride or a haze of greed.

We don't *see*, certainly not clearly and well, and in our fogginess we set out on courses that are all wrong for us.

I see it happening all the time. I talk with X., who is making only mediocre grades (by dint of tremendous effort) but who wants to become a professor of political science. I talk with Y., who has a serious speech defect but who wants to become a priest. I talk with Z., who wants to be a successful sculptor but whose work, which seems clumsy even to me, has been rejected by every gallery within five hundred miles.

Each of these people has other gifts, great gifts. But the pity is that their gifts are not being identified, cultivated, employed.

My heart goes out to people like X. and Y. and Z. I want to say to them, "Look, why don't you switch to something else? Something more in line with who and what you really are." But all too often, unfortunately, a questionable kindness or outright timidity—or both—compels me to hold my tongue.

> The responses a child gets from those around him gradually move inside him and become a conscious or unconscious conviction about himself: *I am like that*. This happens for better or worse: for better, if the self-image to which he thus commits himself is fairly realistic, so that it encourages him to develop and use the powers he has; for worse, however, if the image is grossly unrealistic. In that event, he will tend toward a state of inner conflict, where he is always hitting himself over the head for being such a dope; and of outer conflict, where he is always hitting the world over the head for not agreeing with him about himself: for asking too much of him, or not putting a proper value upon him, or not recognizing his need to be comforted and looked after.
>
> No human being finds it altogether easy to "put away childish things." But the victim of a false self-image finds it abnormally hard. The task he has unwittingly cut out for himself—that of being what he is not— condemns him to repeated disappointment and failure. His anxiety increases; his attention turns in more and more upon himself; and he misses more and more of the objective clues that might help him both to rectify his self-estimate and to make successful responses to his environment. The emotional fatigue and despair thus generated in him

work to exaggerate the normal human nostalgia for childhood's free country to a point where it becomes an all-consuming desire.[5]

—Harry and Bonaro Overstreet

On self-acceptance . . .

I heard a man say yesterday, "Ministers are *called*—a chosen group. They're different, they're special."

Different? I don't think so. Ministers are human—just as human, in fact, as bus drivers, brain surgeons, and bee keepers. Ministers, too, are subject to anger and depression and lust and greed. But not, of course, in public.

> I remember an amusing tale from the days of one of my early pastorates, about the minister of a rural church nearby. It seems that the minister had arisen rather late on Sunday morning and was grouchily hurrying to get ready for church. As often happens when we are in the greatest haste, everything was going wrong. The minister was getting testier and testier. The climax came when his wife's cat, which he had always disliked rather intensely, scooted across the dresser top to avoid a swat he had aimed at it and sent his tie pin flying under the bed. Completely overcome with anger, the minister seized the cat and flung it against the wall, where it landed in a tight position behind a hot radiator and was greatly singed and disturbed before the minister's wife, hearing the sounds of torture, rushed to the room and rescued it.
>
> Two hours later the minister, now composed and serene, the very soul of gentleness, was standing in the pulpit of his church extolling the many virtues of Christian love. "When I am in Christ," he was saying, "I am possessed of great peace and calm, of a feeling of charity for everyone and everything." Whereupon his wife, who was sitting near the rear of the sanctuary and was possessed not of great peace and calm but of a near frenzy, said in such bitter audibility that nearly everyone in the back ten pews of the church was able to hear her, "Don't you believe him! Don't you believe him! The old hypocrite, you should see what he did to my cat!"[6]
>
> —John Killinger

Ambition, for example. I see as much of it in ministry as I do anywhere else. It isn't perhaps as naked, as raw as it is in other fields, but it is there all the same. I see it in people I know—not many of them, granted, but a few. People who are ever so mindful of their professional image. People who are forever saying and doing the politic thing, cultivating their contacts with influential figures, wangling their way into important committees and jockeying for position in the corridors of power. All of it done, of course, with an eye to the main chance, the next step up the ecclesiastical ladder.

In some cases their dreams are realized; they reach the top, or close to it. In other instances, however, ambitions remain unfulfilled, and bitter disappointment, buttered with acute frustration, becomes their daily bread.

On the other hand, I know a number of people who could be classified as "humble parish priests." People who, whether early or late, have come to accept their limitations and who, in that acceptance, are supremely content in a comparatively modest role.

I think of Albert. Classmates go on from eminence to eminence while he remains in obscurity, the servant of a struggling rural parish. His clothes are old and threadbare. His car is a rust heap. He isn't a particularly tidy person, nor much of an orator. But what he is, nonpareil, is a dear, dear man; a living, breathing, loving benediction to the whole countryside.

Albert is a man totally devoid of ambition. "I like where I am," he says. "I love it." And people love him.

> (Recently, having observed an extraordinarily charming and relaxed doctor, one of us asked him how he avoided Type A behavior. He smiled and said, "A few years ago, I faced up to the truth that I always had been and always will be a second-rate physician. After I realized this, it was quite easy to begin to relax.")[7]
>
> —Meyer Friedman and Ray H. Rosenman

As the very opposite of blind ambition, a clear-eyed self-acceptance is its sovereign cure.

> I had the same dream each night—that I had a child; and even in the dream I saw that the child was my life; and it

was an idiot. And I wept, and a hundred times I ran away, but each time I came back it had the same dreadful face. Until I thought, if I could kiss it, whatever in it was my own, perhaps I could rest. And I bent to its broken face, and it was horrible . . . but I kissed it. . . . I think one must finally take one's life in one's arms, Quentin.[8]

—Arthur Miller

I am convinced that our reluctance to accept ourselves has its roots in our tendency to equate self-acceptance with stagnation. When we accept ourselves, as we see it, we stop growing and start vegetating; we preclude any further personal development; we sentence ourselves to a flat and hopeless existence.

I am also convinced, however, that such feelings are a lie, convinced that while self-acceptance often *seems* to spell the death of our fondest hopes and most glittering dreams, it is actually a prelude to life: We finally accept ourselves and, lo and behold, we spread our wings and begin the ascent into a different but beautiful sky.

When, gradually . . . , he brings his self-image more in line with reality, he begins to savor the peace of self-acceptance. This is no passive peace. It does not express itself in his saying, "I am only what I am—and that's that. I didn't ask to be born. I didn't make myself, and I'm not responsible for the fact that I'm not different." This line of defense belongs, rather, to the stage before the self-image has been rectified—when the individual is still needing explanations and excuses for failure. A genuine self-acceptance works in quite the opposite way. It makes the individual feel, with a new serenity, "Well . . . I am at least what I am. I may not set the world on fire. But I can be myself and see what comes of it."

Such an attitude may seem to mean only that the individual is lowering his sights; unhitching his wagon from a star; accepting mediocrity as his lot. Yet this is not what happens. The valuable effect of the changed attitude is that it releases the individual from his consuming anxiety about himself and lets him do the one thing prerequisite to any realistic dealing with life: namely, *turn his attention outward*. It is this shift in the direction of attention that makes the patient say what he has not said before—and say it more thoughtfully.[9]

—Harry and Bonaro Overstreet

Self-acceptance is not entire if it does not include the acceptance of some extension of oneself—the acceptance of some painfully limiting situation with which the self is totally identified, some situation to which the self is committed "for better or worse" and from which, therefore, there can be no conscientious nor moral disengagement.

One of my idols is Teilhard de Chardin, scientist and mystic both, who died on Easter Sunday, 1955. (A year earlier he had said, "I should like to die on the day of the Resurrection.")

I suspect that even more than most writers, Teilhard wanted to see his work published: He was way out on the frontiers of human thought, seeing patterns and possibilities no one had ever glimpsed before; he had a vision of the future he wanted to share with the whole world.

Rome, however, decided that his work did not conform to the criteria of faith and decreed that it could not be published.

Totally committed to the Church, Teilhard simply accepted the dictate. There was no protest, no rebellion; there was only acquiescence. "A week ago," he wrote a friend, "I had a letter from my General forbidding me (in a perfectly courteous way) from publishing anything that involved philosophy or theology. And that neatly cuts out a large part of the activity still left open to me. . . . All this isn't making life any brighter. Still, it is forcing me back upon 'the one thing that is necessary.' 'Everything that happens is worthy of worship,' Termier used to say."[10]

Within a decade of his death, the writing was published and the priest world renowned.

As I reflect on Teilhard, I am reminded, as I am when I read the Gospels, that every creative force in the cosmos is on the side of legitimate ambition and that in one way or another, if not in time then in eternity, that ambition will be realized.

12

TIME, INSIGHT, AND LOVE

She has every reason for gratitude: a good marriage, a successful career, a spacious and elegant home. But beneath it all there is a festering sore: She still hates her father. Over a decade after his death, she speaks of him, if at all, with a great deal of bitterness. "True," she says, "he was a good provider, but the fact is that he gave us almost nothing of himself. Everything went into his work. Basically, he was a very selfish man. He just didn't give a damn."

I meet such people from time to time, men and women whose souls are poisoned by the resentments they bear fathers and mothers living and even dead.

I am convinced, though, that until we have forgiven those who are near, if not dear, to us, we are not free to truly love either the wider family of the human race or ourselves.

> Forgiveness is the key to re/creation of the past and the future. Without forgiveness there is only the endless repetition of the cycle of resentment-retaliation-reaction. Injuries must be recognized; pain fully felt; forgiveness offered before anything new can happen. So long as I blame my parents I remain a child.[1]
>
> —Sam Keen

A friend was telling me of his two brothers-in-law, both residents of the same small town. Five years ago the brothers quarreled and stopped speaking to each other. Now, a full half decade later, they still are not speaking.

I can imagine them bumping into each other over and over again—it would be inevitable in a small town. I can imagine it happening on Main Street, at a P.T.A. meeting, in the post office, or, for all I know, even in church.

How, I wonder, do they handle those encounters? Do they feel awkward? Embarrassed? Ashamed? Surely there must be at least a little discomfiture and strain, not to mention the cumulative wear and tear on the human spirit.

> A classic case of this sort involved a man who got so mad at his wife that he refused to say one single word to her for 18 months. . . . During this entire period the man lived and worked normally, came home on time, ate a silent dinner and retired with his wife—who must have been a formidable character herself—to a silent bed. After intensive family counseling the husband finally broke his marathon silence. His very first words were, "I DON'T WANT TO TALK ABOUT IT!"[2]
>
> —Shana Alexander

A month after their marriage, his wife confessed that eight years earlier she had had an affair with another man. Instead of putting it out of his mind, he brooded for almost twenty years on his wife's premarital involvement, then exploded. He flew halfway across the continent, went to the home of his wife's ex-lover, and flung several ounces of acid in the man's face, hospitalizing him for eighteen days.

I can see resenting someone for days, weeks, perhaps even months on end. But twenty years? No, twenty years is too long to nurse a grudge. In fact, a day is too long. As André Maurois put it, "Life is too short to be little."

In its own twisted way, hatred is a form of homage. After all, we don't hate our inferiors. We may ridicule and disparage them, may scorn and despise them. But hate them? No, hatred is a tribute we reserve for our equals and superiors.

A cichlid, a perchlike tropical fish, is friendly with his mate only so long as there is another male cichlid around, a fish at which he can scowl menacingly. Even a mirror in his aquarium is a suitable substitute—given that, he can scowl at himself. But if the other male is removed, or the mirror becomes dirty, the essentially nasty cichlid promptly devours his mate.

We see the cichlid in the world of literature, people with a strange need for someone to hate.

Somerset Maugham told of two men who had been confined in a sanitarium for years and who spent every day of life complaining about each other, competing for privileges and annoying the hell out of one another. Then, however, one of the men died and the other was brokenhearted. Deprived of his enemy, he saw no point in going on.

Elizabeth Salter said of Edith Sitwell, with whom she had worked closely for several years, "Crises were the order of the day, but she needed her crises as she needed her pests."[3] Pests for Dame Edith were those bothersome people who, in getting her adrenalin going, gave her a new lease on life. (Yet, said her biographer, there was no doubt that this unnatural stimulation "took its toll.")

We see the cichlid in people we know personally, people for whom hatred is a source of meaning and satisfaction, if not, in fact, their whole raison d'être. Remembering, we may even see the cichlid in our wartime selves. Remember the collective hatred, if not of the Nazi and Jap, then certainly of the cause they represented? It was a hatred that helped fuel our drive. Only, of course, we didn't call it hatred; we called it patriotism.

> I knew a woman once who was dying of a tragic disease, and after several years of lingering with her in the never-never land between life and death, her husband chose life and left.
>
> It was a very hard decision for him to make, but he left nevertheless, and started a new life for himself, one that included children and a new wife. His former wife, left alone, had nothing left when he departed, nothing but her memories and her anger.
>
> And every day the anger grew. She forbade her friends to see him, and she made everyone she knew choose between them and cut off those who would not censor him. Some days she spent all her energy dialing, with the pencil held between her teeth, the number of his office, so she could call him and complain, and other days she exhausted herself dictating her story into a tape recorder so that she could tell it to the world and make him an object of shame.
>
> The nurses who looked after her hated to see her so upset and tried to calm her down, but she resisted all their efforts and continued to fan the flames. And finally, they came to understand that anger was all she had to live for, and it had become a substitute for love.[4]
>
> —Merle Shain

Hatred is a fierce desire to achieve equality or, better, superiority by simultaneously tearing one's enemy down and building oneself up.

Hatred is all too often a justification for, as we see it, our mediocrity or failure. A son says, or implies, of his more successful father, "It's all because of him that I've had such a hell of a time; it's because of parental neglect." (For "neglect," of course, we can substitute cruelty, ignorance, rotten genes, or whatever else.)

Tolstoy. All five of his sons were "weaklings and wastrels," a spoiled, dissolute crew who bitterly resented their father. Said Andrei, "If I were not his son, I would hang him."[5] Lev, an aspiring writer but with only a fraction of his father's talent, was even more venomous than his younger brother. Lev swore at his father, derided his values, and eventually sought to have him declared mentally incompetent.

Gandhi. His eldest child, Harilal, consorted with prostitutes, fell into embezzlement, was converted to Islam out of sheer spite, vilified his father all over India, and died (only five months after the Mahatma himself) a gaunt, toothless derelict, ravaged by alcoholism and tuberculosis.

> I think some people cling to anger because to have been wronged makes them feel right. And they recite the horrors done to them as if they were saying a prayer inviting the gods to give them points for each wrong that they've endured. So important is it to them to confirm their rightness, that they dust off their hurts as often as they can and polish them until they gleam—feeling somehow that by so doing they have earned their keep. And they puff themselves up with their moral indignation like a child clings to a teddy bear for protection in the dark of the night.
>
> It's as if they feel that if there is a bad guy, there must also be a good guy, and the worse the other guy is the better that makes them. And like the person who needs a triumph a day to keep his angst about his own powerlessness away, the person who believes in good guys and bad guys always needs a bad guy to affirm himself.[6]
>
> —Merle Shain

When I hate someone, I become that person's subject; I allow him or her to determine my mood, my behavior, the whole tone and tenor of my life. I refuse to so demean myself.

Hatred diminishes, damages, deranges, and even destroys us.

"Hate," said Schiller, "is a prolonged form of suicide."

Prolonged? Not necessarily.

Early in my ministry I preached a sermon questioning the Virgin Birth. I was dead wrong, wrong not so much in what I said as in the way I said it, wrong in my arrogance and insensitivity, and I am largely to blame for the consequences: An elderly, conservative parishioner was so incensed by my loveless ultraliberalism that she went home and suffered a stroke from which she died only a few days later.

Shortly before she died, I went to see her in the hospital. She was speechless, her face all twisted and awry. Her eyes, though, were eloquent with fury. "I hate you!" she cried, speechless. "I hate you for what you said and now for *this*!"

I have never forgotten that look. Nor have I forgiven myself for being the cause of such a fierce and destructive hatred.

In a lighter vein . . .

An old-timer in Muskoka swears this is the truth, and we pass it on as a timely warning to city dwellers once again bravely setting off for northern cottages. *This* cottager had settled in and was entertaining his first group of weekend guests around a campfire by the shore when he discovered a porcupine rattling around in a nearby tree. Announcing he was going to rid himself of a pest that had eaten a dozen holes in his cottage, he left the convivial fireside, obtained a small revolver and scrambled up after the beast. Climbing within range of the porky, he stood on one branch, hung firmly to a branch overhead with his left hand, aimed with his right and fired. It was a dead shot. He winged his own left hand, killed the porcupine, tumbled after his enemy to the ground and landed square on top of it. The hunter ended up in hospital for repairs to his hand, three broken ribs, and a badly punctured seat.[7]

"Hatred," said someone, "does more harm to the vessel in which it is stored than to the object on which it is poured."

Among the remedies for hatred, as I see it, are time, insight, and, supremely, love.

Time . . .

We were in Grade 9 at the time. Playing ball during the noon-hour one day, we quarreled.

"Want to settle this after school?" he challenged.

"Sure," I said with false bravado.

We met in a vacant lot. Around us were at least fifty others, all eager to see us do battle. Clearly, the word had spread. "Fight, fight! Ashford and J_________. After four."

He battered me into broken, bloody submission. When I wakened the next morning, I was so bruised and stiff I could scarcely move.

I hated him, not only for the physical punishment he had inflicted but also for the public humiliation.

At the end of that school year, our paths diverged. He went one way and I another.

I next saw him almost twenty years later. But where life had been good to me in that long interval, it had been painfully hard on him; it had turned out a worn, subdued little man, poorly dressed and condemned, apparently, to a future no better than his past.

I felt sorry for him. Granted, my pity was not the equal of love. Still, it was a far cry from the hatred I had once felt. Hatred would have been impossible. How could I hate someone who had fared so badly?

More time passed, and I felt the same sorrow for my father. Only now, because it was Dad, the sorrow was more deeply felt. Once I had resented him, but as I watched him age, as I saw increasingly the frailty and confusion—and as I aged myself—the resentment turned to pity, the pity to compassion, and the compassion to love.

Time, it seems, is on the side of forgiveness. Time changes not only people but also our view of people. Time heals and resolves and blesses. Time is an instrument of grace.

> Our attitude to all men would be Christian if we regarded them as though they were dying, and determined our relation to them in the light of death, both of their death and of our own. A person who is dying calls forth a special kind of feeling. Our attitude to him is at once softened and lifted on to a higher plane. We then can feel compassion for people whom we did not love. But every man is dying. I too am dying and must never forget about death.[8]
>
> —Nicholas Berdyaev

Insight . . .

Like so many poets and philosophers, Tagore, the Hindu poet, was hopelessly inept when it came to cooking meals, tidying up, sewing on buttons, and doing other such household chores. He solved his problems by hiring a servant. One morning, however, the servant failed to appear. An hour went by, and Tagore was getting angrier by the minute. Another three hours passed, and, furious, he was no longer thinking of possible punishments; he was going to fire the man with no further ado. Finally, around noon, the servant arrived and went to work as though nothing had happened. Tagore exploded: "Drop everything and get out!" Still silent, the servant went on sweeping, then explained with quiet dignity, "My little girl died last night."

I have made the same mistake myself. I have jumped to merciless conclusions. I have seethed and condemned, but without knowing all the facts.

Once, I remember, I went into a small store to buy a special light bulb. Inside, everything was dingy and quiet; I was the only customer. Moments later the storeowner, a thin, middle-aged man, emerged silently from a room at the back. I told him what I wanted. "Don't have it," he said curtly, then turned and walked away. I was furious. "From now on," I fumed to myself, "I'll take my business elsewhere!"

A few days later I learned that the storeowner was dead. He had come home from work and in a bleak, empty house gone downstairs and hanged himself from the basement ceiling.

I was shocked and sick at heart, ashamed because I had been so critical of a broken, defeated man. If only, I thought, I had not been so obtuse. If only I had made a few allowances, made even the slightest effort to understand. If only I and others had been a little kinder . . .

A few years ago I drove from coast to coast, interviewing scores of people who had known my father. A biography was what I had in mind, the story of an extraordinarily vital and colorful man. In the course of all those interviews, I came to see more and more clearly something I had only glimpsed before. I saw that Dad, whom I had once faulted, was by no means entirely to blame for his parental deficiencies. I saw that he himself had suffered from poor parenting, as no doubt had his father before him, and his grandfather before that again, and so on, for all I knew, ad infinitum. I saw that actually my father was only one in a long line of victims, and I remembered the old, old law that speaks of "visiting the iniquity of the fathers upon the children to the third and the fourth generation."[9]

It has often happened. Whether suddenly or gradually, I have come to see the reasons for a person's behavior and so to accept and forgive.

"Know all," said Thomas à Kempis in his *Imitation of Christ*, "and you will pardon all."

It follows, I think, that a harsh, punitive Deity is out of the question. If God is infinitely wise, he must also be infinitely merciful and kind.

Love . . .

I remember the first time Phyl kissed me. I was so elated, so overcome with joy that on the way home, singing soundless paeans of praise to the powers that be, I could gladly have embraced a Genghis Khan.

I have known other moments, too, when my heart was so full of love that there was no room for even an atom of resentment.

Speaking of those rare, transcendent moments when love takes total possession, Elizabeth Byrd wrote:

> There was nothing extraordinary about the day as it began. I awakened as usual at 9 o'clock in my bedroom facing New York's East 11th Street. There were the familiar city sounds: the banging of trash cans, rattle of traffic, blare of a neighbor's television. It was July 30, 1959.

As I stretched and yawned I moved mentally through the day ahead. There would be the usual six or seven hours of work on my novel; a beauty parlor engagement at 4 P.M.; a dinner date at seven. I must stress again that there was nothing unusual in any of this. It was a perfectly ordinary day.

In my robe I went through the living room to the kitchen, put on water for coffee and drank a glass of orange juice. Then, suddenly, I was struck by what I can only call an "awareness"—a moment nearly indescribable, a moment so emotionally shattering that I sat down on the kitchen stool, unable to stand.

It was as if, in that brief moment, all the love in the world was beamed on me and I returned it with such intense joy that my eyes streamed tears. I was cradled in the universe, loved by every living thing, based in wind and rain, sea and star. Time seemed nonexistent, but I doubt if the experience lasted more than 10 ecstatic seconds. Because, when it vanished, as suddenly as it had come, the water for coffee was not yet boiling.[10]

—Elizabeth Byrd

It wasn't something I had been working and hoping for; it was a visitation, a gift that came as the most overwhelming surprise of my life. It came not at, say, sunset on a Caribbean island, a place consistent with the gift itself; it came on a drab downtown street, a place of littered gutters and grimy old buildings.

I was hurrying along, preoccupied with some minor matter, when suddenly I was so "possessed by love," so engulfed in a great wave of ecstasy, flooding every part of my being, that for those few timeless moments I was oblivious to the street, the buildings, the sky, everything. I was aware only of Love and, vaguely, the people around, whom I longed to include in that Love. In fact, drawing on the last remnants of a sense of propriety, I was barely able to keep from throwing my arms around those dim figures, total strangers, in an attempt to gather them into the dazzling, transcendent Love that had charged my whole universe.

I have never since experienced Love in all its fullness. But I know now that Love is there, waiting in the wings, and that when its moment comes, nothing on earth, least of all our petty resentments, can resist its force.

NOTES

Chapter 1: "I Like My Wrinkles"

1. Simone de Beauvoir, *Old Age* (London: André Deutsch and George Widenfeld and Nicolson, 1972), p. 283.
2. Monica Furlong, *Travelling In* (London: Hodder and Stoughton, 1971), p. 60.
3. Garson Kanin, *It Takes a Long Time to Become Young* (New York: Berkley Books, 1978), p. 84.
4. Source unavailable.
5. John W. Gardner and Francesca Gardner Reese, eds., *Quotations of Wit and Wisdom* (New York: W. W. Norton, 1975), p. 44.
6. Jim Watters quoting Anita Loos in *People*; quoted in turn in "Points to Ponder," *Reader's Digest*, Aug. 1982, p. 110.
7. Simone de Beauvoir, *Old Age*, p. 305.
8. Garson Kanin, *It Takes*, p. 43.
9. Viktor Frankl, *Man's Search for Meaning* (Boston: Beacon, 1962), p. 26.
10. *Encyclopedia of World Art* (New York: McGraw-Hill, 1963), Vol. 7, Column 584.
11. Simone de Beauvoir, *Old Age*, p. 540.
12. John A. B. MacLeish, *The Ulyssean Adult: Creativity in the Middle and Later Years* (Toronto: McGraw-Hill Ryerson, 1976), p. 246.
13. Lillian Eichler Watson, ed., *Light from Many Lamps* (New York: Simon and Schuster, 1951), p. 269.

Chapter 2: Nonpossessive Parents

1. Loral Dean, "Throwaway Kids," *Today*, Nov. 8, 1981, p. 10.
2. Kahlil Gibran, *The Madman: His Parables and Poems* (London: Heinemann, 1963), pp. 15-16.
3. David McCullough, "Mama's Boys," *Psychology Today*, March 1983, p. 34.
4. 2 Samuel 18:31-33.
5. John 3:16.
6. As quoted in Lewis Thomas, *The Medusa and the Snail* (New York. Bantam Books, 1980), p. 14.

7. Kahlil Gibran, *The Prophet* (New York: Alfred A. Knopf, 1955), pp. 17-18.

Chapter 3: In Praise of Foolishness

1. Ram Dass, *Journey of Awakening* (New York: Bantam Books, 1978), p. 5.
2. James Sutherland, ed., *The Oxford Book of Literary Anecdotes* (New York: Coward, McCann and Geoghegan, 1976), p. 306.
3. Elizabeth Goudge, ed., *A Book of Faith* (New York: Coward, McCann and Geoghegan, 1976), p. 306.
4. Joseph C. McLelland, *The Clown and the Crocodile* (Richmond, Va.: John Knox, 1970), pp. 11-12.
5. C. S. Lewis, *The Four Loves* (New York: Harcourt, Brace, 1960), pp. 140-141.
6. Sam Keen, *To a Dancing God* (New York: Harper & Row, 1970), pp. 117-119.

Chapter 4: The Frugality Phenomenon

1. Edmund Fuller, ed., *Affirmations of God and Man* (New York: Association, 1967), p. 132.
2. Anne Morrow Lindbergh, *Gift from the Sea* (New York: Pantheon Books, 1955), pp. 30-34.
3. Duane Elgin, *Voluntary Simplicity* (New York: Bantam Books, 1982), p. 2.
4. Marilyn Ferguson, *The Aquarian Conspiracy* (Los Angeles: J. P. Tarcher, 1980), p. 40.
5. Richard J. Foster, *Freedom of Simplicity* (New York: Harper & Row, 1981), p. 170.
6. Ibid., p. 127.

Chapter 5: "I'm Uncomfortable Around Gods"

1. Editors, *The Community* (New York: Time-Life Books, 1976), p. 73.
2. Hugh Prather, *Notes to Myself* (New York: Bantam Books, 1976).
3. *The Concise Oxford Dictionary.*
4. Aaron J. Ungersma, *Escape from Phoniness* (Philadelphia: Westminster, 1969), p. 62.
5. Leo Rosten, *Infinite Riches* (New York: McGraw-Hill, 1979), p. 510.
6. Ibid., p. 511.

7. Dan Dillany and David Dowie, *The Cage* (Panther), quoted in Monica Furlong, *Travelling In* (London: Hodder and Stoughton, 1971), pp. 77-78.

Chapter 6: The Courage to Love

1. William Barclay, *Seen in the Passing* (London: Collins, 1966), p. 30.
2. Bruce Larson, *The One and Only You* (Waco, Tex.: Key-Word Books, 1976), pp. 18-19.
3. Jacques Prévert, "Early Breakfast," tr. William E. Baker (New York: Twayne, 1967), quoted in Jean Vanier, *Eruption to Hope* (Toronto: Griffin House, 1971), p. 23.
4. David A. MacLennan, *No Coward Soul* (Toronto: Clarke, Irwin, 1949), p. 181.
5. W. T. McLeod, ed., *Dictionary of Quotations* (London: Collins, 1961), p. 423.
6. William Barclay, *A Spiritual Autobiography* (Grand Rapids, Mich.: William B. Eerdmans, 1977), pp. 35-36.
7. Smiley Blanton, "The Magic of Touch," *Guideposts*, Aug. 1965, p. 23.
8. Grace Stuart, *Narcissus* (London: Geo. Allen and Unwin, 1956), p. 38.

Chapter 7: Let Go and Let God

1. C. S. Lewis, *Surprised by Joy* (New York: Harcourt, Brace, 1955), p. 226.
2. Ibid., p. 212.
3. Victor Gollancz, ed., *Man and God* (Boston: Houghton Mifflin, 1951), p. 229.
4. Dante Alighieri, *Paradiso*, Bk. III, 1. 85.
5. Dag Hammarskjöld, *Markings* (London: Faber and Faber, 1964), p. 169.
6. John W. Gardner and Francesca Gardner Reese, *Quotations of Wit and Wisdom* (New York: W. W. Norton, 1975), p. 10.
7. Acts 4:12.
8. Emilie Griffin, *Turning* (Garden City, N.Y.: Doubleday, 1980), p. 173.
9. Ibid., pp. 140-141.
10. C. S. Lewis, *The Great Divorce* (New York: Macmillan, 1959), p. 66.
11. C. S. Lewis, *The Problem of Pain* (London: Geoffrey Bles, 1950), pp. 78-80.

12. As quoted in Emilie Griffin, *Turning*, pp. 29-30.

Chapter 8: Insufficiency—An Invitation to Love

1. Brian Butters, Southam News, *Windsor Star,* Jan. 24, 1980.

Chapter 9: The Importance of Being Lazy

1. Gerald Kennedy, ed., *A Reader's Notebook* (New York: Harper, 1953), pp. 263-264.
2. Ecclesiastes 2:11.
3. Christopher J. Hegarty, "Do You Work Too Hard? An Expert Explains the Dangers," *U.S. News & World Report*, March 26, 1979, p. 74.
4. Genesis 2:1-2.
5. Rollo May, *The Courage to Create* (New York: W. W. Norton, 1975), pp. 45-46, 61-62.
6. Ray Ashford, *Take It Easy* (Philadelphia: Fortress, 1976), pp. 10-16.

Chapter 10: Love Lets Go

1. H. Allen Smith, *Don't Get Perconel with a Chicken* (Montreal: Permabooks, 1959), pp. 78-79.
2. James J. Lynch, *The Broken Heart* (New York: Basic Books, 1977), pp. 199-200.
3. C. S. Lewis, *The Four Loves* (New York: Harcourt, Brace, 1960), p. 169.
4. David Hendin, *Death As a Fact of Life* (New York: Warner Paperback Library, 1974), pp. 83-84.
5. Robert E. Kavanaugh, *Facing Death* (Baltimore: Penguin Books, 1974), pp. 75-78.
6. W. Scott Peck, *The Road Less Travelled* (New York: Touchstone Books, Simon and Schuster, 1978), p. 98.
7. C. S. Lewis, *The Four Loves*, pp. 91, 98.
8. Carl Seaburg, ed., *Great Occasions* (Boston: Beacon, 1968), p. 111.
9. Robert Runcie, *Time*, Aug. 10, 1981, p. 18.
10. Anne Morrow Lindbergh, *Gift from the Sea* (New York: Pantheon Books, 1955), p. 104.
11. Anne Morrow Lindbergh, "Even—," *The Unicorn and Other Poems* (New York: Pantheon Books, Random House, 1956), pp. 13-14.

Chapter 11: Good-bye to Galloping Ambition

1. J. Wallace Hamilton, *Ride the Wild Horses* (Westwood, N.J.: Fleming H. Revell, 1952), p. 26.
2. Søren Kierkegaard, *The Gospel of Suffering,* tr. D. F. and L. M. Swenson (Minneapolis: Augsburg, 1948), pp. 178-183.
3. June Callwood, *Love, Hate, Fear, Anger* (Garden City, N.Y.: Doubleday, 1964), p. 83.
4. Mark 10:35-37.
5. Harry and Bonaro Overstreet, *The Mind Alive* (New York: W. W. Norton, 1954), pp. 60-61.
6. John Killinger, *For God's Sake, Be Human* (Waco, Tex.: Word Books, 1970), p. 20.
7. Meyer Friedman and Ray H. Rosenman, *Type A Behavior and Your Heart* (Greenwich, Conn.: Fawcett, 1974), p. 220.
8. Arthur Miller, *After the Fall* (New York: Viking, 1964), p. 24.
9. Harry and Bonaro Overstreet, *The Mind Alive,* pp. 67-68.
10. Jeanne Mortier and Marie-Louise Aboux, eds., *Teilhard de Chardin Album* (New York: Harper & Row, 1966), p. 178.

Chapter 12: Time, Insight, and Love

1. Sam Keen, *Beginnings Without End* (New York: Harper & Row, 1975), p. 21.
2. Shana Alexander, "Fight Promoter for the Battle of the Sexes," *Life,* May 17, 1963.
3. Bernard Mobbs, *Our Rebel Emotions* (New York: Seabury, 1970), p. 78.
4. Merle Shain, *The Hearts That We Broke Long Ago* (Toronto: McLelland and Stewart, 1983), pp. 36-37.
5. Martin Green, *Tolstoy and Gandhi, Men of Peace* (New York: Basic Books, 1983), p. 253.
6. Merle Shain, *The Hearts,* pp. 91-92.
7. "Parade," *Maclean's,* May 20, 1961, p. 59.
8. Gerald Kennedy, *A Second Reader's Notebook* (New York: Harper, 1959), p. 333.
9. Exodus 20:5.
10. Elizabeth Byrd, "One Blinding Moment," *Guideposts,* April 1967, p. 26.